1 MONTH OF
FREE
READING

at
www.ForgottenBooks.com

By purchasing this book you are eligible for one month membership to ForgottenBooks.com, giving you unlimited access to our entire collection of over 1,000,000 titles via our web site and mobile apps.

To claim your free month visit: www.forgottenbooks.com/free979831

ISBN 978-0-260-87869-4
PIBN 10979831

This book is a reproduction of an important historical work. Forgotten Books uses
state-of-the-art technology to digitally reconstruct the work, preserving the original format
whilst repairing imperfections present in the aged copy. In rare cases, an imperfection in
the original, such as a blemish or missing page, may be replicated in our edition. We do,
however, repair the vast majority of imperfections successfully; any imperfections that
remain are intentionally left to preserve the state of such historical works.

FOREIGN AGRICULTURE CIRCULAR

OFFICE OF FOREIGN AGRICULTURAL RELATIONS
UNITED STATES DEPARTMENT OF AGRICULTURE
WASHINGTON, D.C.

WFP-1-51   FEBRUARY 8, 1951

FOR RELEASE FEBRUARY 12, 1951

WORLD

FOOD SITUATION

1951

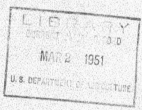

THIS CIRCULAR IS A CONTINUATION OF THE WORLD
FOOD SUMMARIES WHICH HAVE BEEN ISSUED BY THE
OFFICE OF FOREIGN AGRICULTURAL RELATIONS SINCE
1945. IT SUMMARIZES THE FOOD SUPPLY SITUATION
IN MAJOR DEFICIT AND SURPLUS PRODUCING AREAS,
REVIEWS PRODUCTION AND TRADE OF THE MOST
ESSENTIAL FOOD COMMODITIES FOR 1950-51, AND
PRESENTS THE OUTLOOK FOR WINTER CROPS IN THE
NORTHERN HEMISPHERE.

INDEX TO

WORLD FOOD SITUATION 1950-51

Approved by Outlook and Situation Board

January 31, 1951

World Summary

World food production continued to increase in 1950-51 and on a calorie
basis, aggregate output of important food products is expected to total
about 2 percent above last year and 4 percent above the prewar (1935-39)
average. (See table page 5).

Despite the increased output of food in the past three years, the world
supply has not reached the point where the per capita consumption rate,
in terms of calories, equals the prewar rate, due to the increase in the
world's population. However, in 1950-51, the per capita consumption rate
is expected to reach the highest level since the end of World War II and
in many countries it will be close to, or above, prewar. Furthermore,
the quality of diets generally has improved in the postwar period and
in some countries it is better than before the war.

Prior to the crisis in Korea there was growing evidence that the supply
of several food products might soon be in excess of effective demand and
the trend of prices was pointing downward. The impact of that crisis on
the economy of many nations has considerably modified this outlook. The
earlier concern about possible surpluses of certain products has virtually
disappeared, and world prices of many foods have made marked advances.
In many countries, both importing and exporting, consideration now is
being given to the problems of promoting production, building adequate
reserves of essential food products, controlling prices and distributing
available supplies among nations in order to support current military
and rearmament programs.

Situation by Areas

In the United States, production and consumption of food and feed products
continued on high levels in 1950. Exports, though less than in 1949,
remained much larger than before the war.

Per capita consumption of food is at an all-time high in all but a few
Latin American countries. Argentine exports in 1950 were reduced not
only by drought but also by the suspension of meat exports to the United
Kingdom in the middle of the year, following failure to reach an agreement on prices.

The production and consumption of food and feed products in the major
food surplus producing countries of the British Commonwealth also were
maintained on high levels in spite of unfavorable weather conditions in
Canada and Australia which adversely affected the size and quality of
the wheat crop. Normal exports of livestock products from these countries have been somewhat reduced by increased domestic consumption and
by price negotiation difficulties with the United Kingdom.

In the United Kingdom, the world's largest food importer, the level of
production and imports of most food products in 1950 was somewhat higher
and contributed to a further improvement of the food situation. However,

inability to obtain adequate meat imports at desired prices has caused
a reduction in meat rations to the lowest level since rationing was
introduced.

Production and consumption levels in most Continental European countries
have also continued to increase, although a severe drought in 1950 reduced production materially in most of the Danube Basin region. Acute
food shortages have occurred in Yugoslavia, normally an important grain
producing and exporting country, and substantial quantities of grain are
being imported this season to help prevent serious distress. Exportable
grain surpluses from the other East European countries (excluding the
Soviet Union) are also expected to be smaller this year than last.

The food situation in the Soviet Union has improved compared with the
tight situation that prevailed during the War and early post-war period,
but the harvest of principal grains in 1950 is estimated to have been
slightly less than in 1949. Grain export commitments for the 1950-51
season, as of January 15, 1951, amounted to about 1.7 million tons compared with estimated exports of around 1.5 million in 1949-50.

Growing conditions generally were favorable in the Middle East countries
and the 1950 harvest of all but a few crops was unusually good. This
season, the area as a whole should be about self-sufficient in breadgrains,
in contrast to a large deficit in 1949-50. It will have slightly larger
export surpluses of rice and dates.

In the Far East, India is faced with a deteriorating food situation. Crop
output has been cut by floods and droughts, and a large increase in grain
imports is needed to prevent serious distress. In most other parts of
the Far East production is above 1949-50 but in a number of countries political disturbances or transportation difficulties continue to prevent
the regular movement of supplies from surplus to deficit areas, thereby
impeding progress toward the restoration of prewar food consumption levels.

Situation by Commodities

For the world as a whole, production of all important grains except rye
and corn is estimated to be larger in 1950-51 than in the preceding year.
Although the 1950 production of corn was 5 percent below 1949, it was
11 percent above prewar. The 1950 production of breadgrains (wheat and
rye) is expected to be only slightly below the record harvest in 1948.

The 1950-51 crop of rice is one of the largest since World War II, exceeding both the 1949-50 harvest and the prewar average by about 2 percent. Asia's production, representing 92 percent of the world total,
gained more than 2 million tons over 1949 due primarily to the more favorable crop conditions in China and the increased acreage harvested in
Thailand. Drought in northeastern India cut Asia's total production substantially below earlier expectations.

World production of edible fats and oils reached a new post-war peak in
1950, exceeding 1949 by 2 percent and prewar by 4 percent, but on a per
capita basis it has not attained the prewar level. Price rises since
June have aggravated the problem of procurement in dollar areas by countries which are still short of dollar exchange.

World sugar production reached a record level in 1950-51 exceeding last year's record by 10 percent and the prewar average by 22 percent. Europe and Asia produced a smaller proportion of the total sugar output in 1950 than in 1935-39 while North America and other countries produced a greater proportion. Sugar is the only major food crop for which the per capita production is above prewar.

World livestock numbers continued their upward trend in 1950 following three generally favorable seasons for forage and feed supplies. World meat production in 1950 reached a record level, and some further increase is expected in 1951. The output in Europe increased sharply and accounted for nearly all the gain over 1949. In North and South American countries and New Zealand, output increased slightly while in Australia it was slightly lower. Although total meat supplies are 10 percent above prewar, the per capita consumption was still below prewar, except in a few of the important livestock producing countries such as the United States, Canada, and Argentina.

Milk production in 1950 in the important dairy countries of the world, is estimated to be 8 percent larger than prewar and fluid consumption in most countries is reported to be at, or above, prewar levels. Production is expected to increase further in 1951. Surplus stocks of dairy products, especially butter and cheese stocks held by the United States, have practically disappeared in all principal producing countries.

Reports from major producing countries indicate an increase of approximately 5 percent in output of eggs in 1950, compared with 1949 and over 30 percent compared with prewar. The sharp increase from the prewar period is accounted for largely by the 66 percent gain in United States output which reached a high level during World War II and has been maintained since then. However, slight gains have been made in other reporting countries, also.

World production of deciduous fruit is the largest in the post-war period. Increases over last season in apple and grape production more than offset slight decreases in other types of deciduous fruits.

World citrus production in the 1950-51 season shows considerable recovery from the relatively low levels of the last two crop years and is well above the 1935-39 average. The greatest increase over recent years was in oranges and grapefruit as groves recovered from the severe freeze damage that occurred in recent years in a number of important areas and as new groves planted in other areas came into bearing.

The crop of potatoes harvested in 1950-51 exceeded the 1949-50 crop by about 500 million bushels and the prewar average by about 300 million. It is, however, slightly smaller than the huge crop produced in 1948-49. Total world pulse production estimated at 14.5 million tons is lower than in the last few years but approximately 15 percent higher than the prewar average. Rearmament programs now under way in a number of countries have increased economic activity and the expansion of employment and money income is likely to maintain or stimulate the demand for farm products in many areas. The increase in world requirements for both food and industrial raw materials has strengthened the international buying power of a number of food importing countries in Asia, Latin America and Africa. In general, however, it should be noted that, while conditions of full employment accompanying vast rearmament programs tend to increase demand for consumer goods, over a longer period the effect of such programs must be to reduce the production and consequently the consumption of consumer goods including food.

Outlook

Prospects for winter crops in the Northern Hemisphere are variable. In a number of Western European countries, particularly in the British Isles and the Scandinavian countries, excessive rains during the fall of 1950 delayed fall seeding operations which will result in some reduction of 1951 acreage, unless the acreage of spring-sown crops is increased. The condition of crops in the Mediterranean area was reported good at the beginning of January. The drought in the Balkan area was reported broken in October, facilitating fall seeding. Some increase in acreage of fall-sown crops is reported for the Soviet Union. The United States winter wheat acreage is estimated 6 percent above a year ago. Dry contions in the important southern Great Plains area have been unfavorable for development of the crop there, but in most other areas the conditions of the crop appeared mostly satisfactory at midwinter.

Food production in many areas has been encouraged to high levels during the past several years and further gains will be increasingly difficult to attain. There will be greater demands upon factors of production such as labor, raw materials for machinery, and chemicals, important in agriculture as well as in the defense industries, which may forestall further basic increases in farm output in countries of intensive cultivation. In fact, it may not be possible to maintain the levels now reached. On the other hand, improved agricultural techniques developed during the past decade could be applied more widely and greater production attained if proper incentives are present. On balance, it would appear, however, that unless the international situation eases considerably, there is no substantial prospect now for further general expansion in food production and consumption in the world at large except perhaps in areas where under-employment exists or where the impact of defense preparations is insignificant.

World production of selected food and feed products,
average 1935-39, and annual 1947-50 1/

Products	Unit	Average 1935-39	1947	1948	1949	1950 2/
		(I n	m i	l l i o n s)		
Food						
Rice, milled......	Sh.tons	117.2	115.8	119.7	116.7	119.0
Wheat.............	Bushels	6,024	5,780	6,420	6,270	6,424
Rye..............	"	1,732	1,520	1,670	1,715	1,665
Sugar, centrifugal, raw.............	Sh.tons	29.1	27.8	31.4	32.1	35.5
Sugar, non-centrifugal.....	" "	4.9	5.9	5.9	6.2	5.7
Vegetable oils....	" "	8.4	9.2	8.8	9.6	9.2
Coconut and palm oils.............	" "	3.0	2.3	2.4	2.7	2.8
Animal fats.......	" "	8.3	7.3	7.5	8.2	8.7
Marine oils.......	" "	1.0	.6	.6	.7	.8
Potatoes.........	Bushels	8,303	7,468	8,764	8,062	8,580
Pulses 3/.........	Bags 4/	292	317.0	333.2	332.0	307.8
Deciduous fruits 5/.......	Sh.tons	61.5	55.1	54.6	60.9	61.8
Citrus fruits.....	" "	9.8	13.5	12.3	12.1	13.5
Meat.............	Pounds	67,900	65,500	64,700	68,500	72,700
Milk.............	"	450,000	380,000	390,000	420,000	440,000
Feed						
Corn.............	Bushels	4,750	4,820	6,040	5,565	5,295
Oats.............	"	4,364	3,735	4,200	4,020	4,210
Barley...........	"	2,357	2,190	2,380	2,260	2,430
Total percent of 1935-39 6/	Percent	100	95	101	102	104

1/ Some revisions were made in figures previously
published as additional data became available.
2/ Preliminary.
3/ Beans, peas, lentils, chickpeas (garbanzos).
4/ One bag equals 100 pounds.
5/ Includes apples, pears, peaches, apricots, cherries,
plums and prunes.
6/ Computed by weighting food products by calories available
as food, i.e., deducting allowances for waste in
processing, seed, etc.

BRITISH ISLES

United Kingdom

The 1950 average per capita intake of food on a calorie basis in the
United Kingdom again approximated the prewar level and the variety of
food available more nearly approached the prewar standard than at any
other time since 1939. The domestic food production again increased.
Rationing continues for sugar, fats and oils, cheese, bacon, beef, veal,
mutton and lamb, eggs, and tea. Largely because of difficulty in negotiation of prices, but partly because of increased demand in the producing country, imports of bacon and beef in the last quarter of 1950
were not up to the level in the comparable 1949 period.

There was a notable reduction in the level of meat consumption in the
latter part of the calendar year 1950 and the first part of 1951. For
the year 1950, as a whole, however, the amount of protein available for
civilian consumption in the United Kingdom was greater than at any other
time since before the last war, including the years immediately prior
to 1940. Shipments of carcass meat from Argentina to the United Kingdom
ceased in the third quarter of 1950 due to difficulty in reaching an
agreement on price and other matters, and have not yet been resumed.

In the early part of 1950 milk rationing ended, and during most of the
year supplies of fluid milk have been adequate to satisfy consumer demand.
Eggs were derationed for a part of the year, but reduced imports and a
leveling off of the domestic production necessitated their being again
rationed. The points rationing scheme, which restricted the consumption
of many miscellaneous food items, including various canned foods and
delicacies, was terminated on May 20, except for candy.

Total grain production in the United Kingdom was 7.7 percent lower in
1950 than in 1949. Wheat acreage increased but an adverse harvest season
substantially reduced the amount of millable wheat produced domestically.
Both coarse grain acreage and yields were reduced, causing the output of
coarse grains to drop 16.3 percent below 1949. The hay crop was badly
damaged by the adverse weather, lowering its feeding value.

It has been necessary to continue rationing of feedstuffs during 1950,
and the supply situation is expected to be less satisfactory in the first
half of 1951 than in the corresponding period of 1950. During the 12
months' period beginning December 1950, a maximum of 800,000 long tons
of grain are to be imported from the Soviet Union, compared with 1 million
tons reported to have been received during the previous year. Difficulties
also have been encountered in negotiations with Argentina for grain supplies.

Rains, which adversely affected grain and hay crops in 1950, contributed
to considerably higher yields of root crops and vegetables than were
obtained in 1949. The increase in the potato crop will permit larger-
than-usual amounts for use as livestock feed. The fall marketing of
vegetables estimated at 40 percent above the 1949 level indicates that
the supply of vegetables for 1950-51 is much better than for the previous
year. Size, quality, and perhaps the yield of leading varieties of des-
sert apples were better in 1950 than in 1949. The cooking and cid——

Ireland

Irish production and exports of livestock and livestock products both
continued to expand and there was some shift in the export trade as to
type of product and destination during 1950. Cheese exports were lower
in 1950 than in 1949. Total cattle exports increased about 10 percent
for the 1949-50 crop year, compared with 1948-49. Shipment of store
cattle to the United Kingdom to be fattened declined while the shipments
of fat cattle increased. Since the hay and feed crops of 1950 were
adversely affected by wet weather, and the country is heavily stocked
with cattle, less well-finished cattle may be marketed in 1951.

Consumption in terms of calories remains relatively high. There is,
however, rather heavy consumption of starchy foods, and low fruit
consumption. Tea, sugar, butter, wheat flour, and bread are still
rationed. The quantities obtainable by individual ration-card holders
remained unchanged during the year, but certain restrictions were
applied, particularly in the case of bread and flour, to reduce illegal
usage.

Wheat will be the principal required import food item for 1951. Imported wheat provides approximately one-half of the annual requirements
(estimated at about 550,000 short tons annually). Larger corn imports
will be needed as the supply of certain feed crops, particularly hay,
oats, and mangels, is below average or of inferior quality.

CONTINENTAL EUROPE [1]/ AND FRENCH NORTH AFRICA

Agricultural production in continental Europe and French North Africa in the current year 1950-51 (crops of 1950 and output of livestock products in 1950-51) is expected to be larger than last year and close to the high average for the middle thirties. It will still be several percent short of the record 5-year average (1935-36) through 1939-40. West Europe's index of production is forecast at 108 percent of the average for the middle thirties and East Europe's at 85 percent, or, on a per capita basis, at 95 and 87 percent respectively.

Crops in 1950, for the third year in succession, were grown under unusually favorable weather conditions in most parts of the continent, the only important exception being the Danube Basin region where spring-grown crops especially were hard hit by drought. Fertilizer consumption, already above prewar, showed a further increase, and more agricultural machinery and other farm supplies were available. The area sown to crops, however, still remains below the prewar level. Livestock numbers, though increasing, have not yet fully recovered from their wartime low.

Breadgrain output in 1950, at 92 percent of the 1935-39 average, showed little change as compared with 1949, while coarse grain production fell to 83 percent of the same prewar average, mostly due to a heavy drop in output of corn which is produced mainly in the Danube Basin region. Potato and sugar beet harvests, on the other hand, increased sharply, with sugar beets reaching a record high. The season was generally favorable for both fruits and vegetables. Yields of fodder roots and hay were better than last year, and pastures in most regions were good throughout 1950. Output of livestock products showed a marked upward trend and, if pasture conditions are at least average during the remainder of the 1950-51 season, should exceed the level for 1949-50 when milk, meat and slaughter fat production was within 90 percent of prewar. Any likely increase in slaughter fats, however, will not offset the decrease in other kinds of fats. Olive oil production will be much below last year's high level, and oilseed production is down, especially in the important Danube Basin producing region.

Taking production as a whole, declines are expected only in Greece and in the normally surplus-producing Danube Basin and French North African countries. Elsewhere production probably will show an increase in 1950-51 over 1949-50. As a result, traditionally-deficit West Europe should be able to import less food and still maintain 1949-50 consumption levels. However, it may need to import as much from overseas, since shipments from East Europe, still far below prewar in 1949-50, will be reduced considerably in the current year. Over half of the 1,000,000 short tons of grain shipped out of East Europe (excluding the Soviet Union) in 1949-50, as well as small quantities of sugar, fruits, vegetables, meat and eggs came from the Danube Basin region. This year the region must import food in order to avoid a drastic decline in food consumption.

_____
[1]/ Excluding the Soviet Union

Outside the Danube Basin region consumption levels generally are expected to show some improvement in 1950-51 over 1949-50. Last year consumption, measured in terms of calories, was close to or above the prewar level in most countries, being less than 90 percent of prewar only in Eastern Germany and Spain, and 90-95 percent only in Western Germany and Austria. A tendency to revert to the prewar pattern of consumption was reflected in a widespread decline in consumption of bread and potatoes and increase in consumption of meat, fats, milk, cheese, eggs and sugar. Meat consumption, however, remained well below prewar in most countries, and many also consumed considerably less milk and fats than before the war.

The Food Situation by Regions

The current food situation appears serious in parts of the Danube Basin, notably Yugoslavia where the drought was more severe than in Hungary, Rumania and Bulgaria. Corn, a major food as well as feed grain in the area, was especially hard hit. Even with substantial relief shipments from the United States and such imports as can be obtained elsewhere, the calorie value of Yugoslavia's food supply in 1950-51 may not reach 90 percent of prewar. Reductions in bread rations for city populations varying by categories, but resulting in an overall 10 percent reduction were made, and corn collection quotas were reduced to an average of 43 percent of the original plan and as low as 10 percent in the severely stricken areas. At the end of November the Government prohibited the export of basic foods, such as grain, meat and fats, until July 1, 1951.

Measures have also been taken to restrict consumption in Hungary where the food situation is reported to have become progressively worse during 1950. All food rationing had been abandoned by the end of 1949, but in October 1950 potatoes and onions were placed under controlled distribution, and on January 2, 1951, sugar and flour rationing were reintroduced. Sugar and flour rations are to be sold at controlled prices, and consumers are permitted to buy additional amounts at "commercial" prices. Bulgaria, unlike Hungary, has continued to ration bread during the postwar period. No information is available as to changes in Bulgarian rations. In Rumania, the black bread ration was increased 20 percent in November 1950, and the free sale of white bread at about seven times the price of rationed bread was permitted.

Further north in the other East European countries, the food situation appears to have become somewhat easier. Poland reportedly abandoned all rationing during the course of 1950. The once-severe shortage of meat apparently has been partially alleviated and at the same time exports have been increased, rising in 1950 to over 40,000 short tons, or more than twice the 1949 level. Sugar production amply covers domestic requirements and large export commitments. On the other hand, while Poland exported substantial quantities of grain to the west in 1949-50, it is said to have imported from the Soviet Union about half as much grain as was exported. Czechoslovakia and Eastern Germany are

also said to have received grain from the Soviet Union. In Eastern
Germany most foods remained rationed throughout 1949-50. Potatoes
reportedly were derationed as of September 4, 1950, and bread as of
January 1, 1951. In Czechoslovakia, where bread was derationed in
October 1949, marked shortages of this staple have recently appeared.
Rationing is still maintained for sugar, a major export item, as well
as for meat, fat, milk and eggs.

In the neighboring countries to the west the food situation has
improved materially. Rationing of all foods except sugar was formally
abandoned in Western Germany in March 1950, and sugar was derationed
in the following month. A rapid rise in output of meat and dairy products,
coupled with more liberal treatment of imports, resulted in an especially
sharp increase in the consumption of meats, fats, milk and sugar; except
in the case of sugar, however, the level reached in 1949-50 was still
only about two-thirds of prewar. The improvement in Austria was less
striking but consumption of sugar and animal products there compares
favorably with that in Western Germany. Unlike Western Germany, Austria
still rations sugar and, as of January 1, 1951, reintroduced the suspended
fat ration following some reduction in reserve supplies and a flurry of
hoarding demand in the wake of a Communist scare campaign.

Food consumption levels in Northern Europe are now, as before the
war, the highest on the continent. Sweden has eliminated all food rations
and in 1950 appeared with appreciable exports of breadgrains, butter and
cheese. Denmark, an important surplus producer of livestock products,
derationed butter and margarine late in 1950, but sugar remains rationed
to permit large exports. Norway now rations only sugar, supplies of
which must all be imported, and imported fruit, and Finland only sugar
and margarine.

Consumption in the western continental countries is also at relatively high levels. No foods are rationed in Switzerland, Belgium, the
Netherlands or France. The Netherlands has resumed its traditional role
as an important exporter of milk and dairy products, pork and eggs, though
per-capita consumption of meat and eggs in 1949-50 was only 75 percent
of prewar and below the level prevailing in the other three western
continental countries. France had sizeable net exports of wheat and
meat in 1949-50 when meat consumption was close to the prewar level and
flour consumption, though declining, was still higher than before the war.

Among the Mediterranean countries, Spain is still faced with a
difficult food situation. Though breadgrain supplies are considerably
larger this year than last, they remain well below the level prevailing
prior to the Spanish Civil War, and fat supplies will be down as a
result of the short 1950 olive crop and the small carry-over of oil
from last year. Italy, Greece and Portugal will have about as much food
as last year when consumption was close to the comparatively low prewar
level. Even fat supplies are expected to show little decline, for the
drop in olive oil output should be offset by withdrawals from stocks.
In Italy no food has been rationed since 1949. Spain still rations
bread and olive oil, Greece bread and sugar, and Portugal brown sugar
and unpolished domestic rice.

In French North Africa food supplies should also be as large as last year, but with smaller grain and olive crops the region will have less food for export. In 1949-50, for the first season in the postwar period, French North Africa had an export surplus of wheat, while exports of coarse grain, mostly barley, rose to unusually high levels. Exports of olive oil, nearly all from Tunisia, also rose strikingly and substantially exceeded imports of all fats and oils into the area. All rationing of foodstuffs has now been abandoned.

Crop Prospects for 1951

The 1950-51 growing season in continental Europe did not commence as favorably as the preceding season. November was abnormally wet throughout the north and west and delayed the harvesting of root crops and fall seeding operations. In south and southeastern Europe dry weather delayed planting, though by November most areas had received rain. Weather conditions in French North Africa, on the other hand, favored seeding operations.

Reports on fall-planted acreage indicate a drop in grain acreage in France, the Netherlands, Denmark and Sweden. The drop in Denmark and Sweden is partly offset by an increase in the area under fall-sown oilseeds, whereas in France oilseed acreage shows little change and in the Netherlands the weather was so wet that fall-planted rape fields had to be plowed up in some areas. In western Germany, grain acreage is up slightly and oilseed acreage down. In Italy the fall-sown grain acreage is believed to be about the same as last year, and in Greece some increase is expected.

Judging from these reports and other scattered information it is unlikely that there will be any material increase in the area under fall-sown crops. Even if the area under spring-sown crops is expanded, it would seem optimistic to expect as large a crop output in 1951 as in 1950. Given average weather conditions, crop yields in the Danube Basin should be higher than last year. But west Europe has now enjoyed three above-average years, and some decline in yields is to be expected in 1951.

SOVIET UNION

The food situation in the Soviet Union has improved during the past two years, especially when compared with the severe stringency of the war and early postwar years. It should be borne in mind, however, that information on the food situation of the more remote interior regions of the Soviet Union is scant.

Rationing of foodstuffs was formally abolished in December 1947, coincidental with a drastic devaluation of the Soviet currency. The availability of bread, the principal article of Russian diet and other staples appears to have been satisfactory, but such items as milk, eggs, butter, and sugar have remained in short supply. The inefficiency and inadequacy of the Government-controlled retail distribution system on which the urban population mainly relies, continues to be an adverse factor in the food supply situation.

A further reduction in retail prices of food products sold in Government stores was ordered on March 1, 1950, following a similar step a year earlier. The price of black bread was reduced by 26 percent and of white bread by 30 percent, as compared with a 10 percent reduction on March 1, 1949. Grits was reduced by 15 to 20 percent. The prices of milk and meat, which were not decreased in 1949, were reduced by 10 and 24 to 35 percent, respectively. Despite the successive reductions, prices of foodstuffs in the Soviet Union are still much higher than they were before the war, when they were also high in relation to money incomes. For instance, a kilogram (2.2 pounds) of black bread, the most important staple of Russian diet, which cost 0.85 rubles on January 1, 1940, has been priced since March 1, 1950 at 2 rubles 1/. Similarly, prices of beef were 9 and 21 rubles a kilogram on the respective dates, lamb 14 and 25.50 rubles and milk 2.10 and 3.60 rubles per liter (1.06 quarts), respectively.

The total area of all crops for the 1950 harvest increased by 15 million acres according to an official report and is around 363 million acres compared with an estimated 1938 area for the present Soviet territory of 378 million acres, and the 1950 goal of 392 million acres set by the postwar 5-year plan. A substantial increase took place again in the spring wheat acreage, bringing the total wheat area approximately to its prewar size. The acreages of fiber crops (cotton and flax) were also considerably expanded, and an increase was reported in oilseeds and sugar beet areas.

Weather spotty: The weather situation during the growing season presented a spotty picture. There were complaints of a dry fall in 1949, apparently unfavorable to winter crops in a number of regions. The winter of 1949-50 was characterized by some unusually cold weather, but snow cover was average or better. Spring was early in the European part of the country, but late in Siberia. Moisture conditions were not up to

---

1/ The value of the ruble cannot be stated definitely in terms of United States currency. The official exchange rate of the ruble has been fixed at 18.9 cents United States currency. This rate, however, does not represent the true purchasing power of the ruble, nor does it reflect its depreciation during the war.

expectations in the spring, but rains in June and July were reportedly
very helpful. Indications are that harvesting weather in some regions,
particularly in Siberia, had not been very favorable. An official
Soviet report spoke of unfavorable weather conditions for the grain
crop in "a number of districts of North Caucasus and some other regions
of the country".

A slightly smaller grain crop in 1950 than in 1949 is indicated
by preliminary estimates. Total production of the five principal grains -
wheat, rye, oats, barley, and corn - is roughly estimated at 82.6 million
short tons, compared with 83.4 million tons in 1949 and a 1935-39 average
of 95.6 million tons. The wheat crop alone, however, was up slightly
because of larger acreage. Moreover, the important wheat producing
region of the Ukraine delivered to the Government nearly 45 million
bushels of wheat more than during the preceding season. As to root
crops, indications are that they are as good as, or better, than last
year. According to an official report, total cattle, hogs, horses, sheep
and goats numbers for all types of farms at the end of 1950, were below the
official goals. The numbers of cattle, hogs and horses were still below those
on January 1, 1938, while sheep and goats numbers were considerably above.

As in past years, the Soviet Government has, since the harvest
began, made a strong drive for large and speedy collections of farm
products, especially grain. Pledges to Stalin by farmers in various
districts are embodied in letters published in the Soviet press and
serve to stimulate deliveries. Quotas for the compulsory delivery of
grain and other farm products to the Soviet state are not fixed on
the basis of the size of the crop, but rather on the total land available
for crops, or total acreage on each collective farm. In addition
to the compulsory collections, the Government also obtains grain and
other farm products through payments in kind for work performed on
collective farms by the State machine-tractor stations. Such payments
are at specified rates for each operation per unit of land, but the rates
vary with the officially determined pre-harvest estimates of the crop
in the whole district. The larger volume of work performed by machine-
tractor stations, which were better supplied with tractors, combines and
other machinery in 1950, should increase the supply of grain in the
hands of the Government, provided of course, that the regular delivery
quotas were not reduced.

The outstanding feature of the 1950 grain procurement situation
were more prompt completion and larger procurements as compared with
1949 in the winter wheat-growing Ukraine, and the improvement shown
by the procurement reports from the spring-wheat producing and drought-
ridden Volga area. While the larger procurements in these regions may
be offset to a certain extent by smaller procurements elsewhere, it would
seem that the Soviet Government should have a larger supply of wheat
on hand.

Government Controls Trade: Disposal of this additional grain between
domestic consumption needs, stockpiling and exports depends primarily on
the decision of the Soviet Government, which has a monopoly of all

Soviet foreign trade and controls the great bulk of internal trade.
Thus, at a grain conference in November 1950 held in Geneva, Switzerland
under the auspices of the Economic Commission for Europe, the Soviet
Union indicated that it was not prepared to discuss breadgrains, but
only coarse grains. Total Soviet grain export commitments for 1950-51
season, amounted up to January 15, 1951 to about 1.7 million short
tons, of which less than 460,000 tons (15.9 million bushels) were wheat,
and the rest coarse grains. The United Kingdom is taking more than
half of the total 880,000 short tons of coarse grains. In 1949-50 the
Soviet Union exported around 1.5 million tons of grain.

More rapid progress than in the fall of 1949 was reported in the
sowing of winter crops (wheat and rye) for the 1951 harvest. Unlike the
dry fall of 1949, planting conditions were favorable in the fall of 1950.
Satisfactory wintering of the crops was indicated in the Soviet press
at the end of December. In the northern and central rye-producing
regions, which had spells of cold weather, the snow-cover was adequate
in the middle of January. In the wheat-producing south, where there
was little or no snow, the temperature was fairly high. But lack of
snow-cover in this area, of course, constitutes a source of danger in
case of cold weather during the remainder of the winter and early spring.

MIDDLE EAST .

In general, 1950 was a good agricultural year for the Middle
East. With minor exceptions, growing conditions were favorable, resulting in abundant harvests of the staple food items. Bumper grain
crops were harvested in Turkey, Iraq and Syria, and a good rice crop
in Egypt, with substantial surpluses available for export. With the
exception of Israel, where the citrus crop has not yet recovered from
the serious damage it suffered two years ago, production of exportable
fruits also was good, although total production in Turkey was below
average. The important date crop of Iraq was excellent. Also livestock entered the winter in good shape, promising normal supplies of
meat and other products.

The outstanding exceptions in this promising situation were a
short wheat crop in Egypt, and a much below normal olive crop in
Syria, Lebanon and Israel.

Weather conditions in the fall of 1950 were generally favorable,
and indications are that good crops will be harvested in 1951.

Turkey - Turkey has had good harvests and as a result the food situation in 1950-51 is considerably more favorable than in 1949-50,
which was a poor year. Total grain production appears to be at
least 45 percent higher, with even greater increases in cereals for
human consumption. In contrast with last year, when Turkey was on
a wheat import basis, production of wheat, rye and barley is substantially above domestic requirements. Owing to the serious deple-
tion of grain stocks prior to harvest, it is likely that the bulk
of the present surplus will be retained as insurance against future
crop failures. Additional storage facilities that are available
will induce the Turks to store most of their surplus grain for an
unexpected emergency.

Adequate feed supplies are reflected in more production of milk
and meat per animal, and smaller losses of livestock due to lack of
feed. Pasture conditions also have been favorable. Livestock, eggs,
and cheese will be available for export in amounts about equal to
the average of previous years.

The olive crop prospects are very good; a total output of about
55,000 short tons and an exportable surplus of 12,000 short tons of
olive oil is forecast.

Oilseed prospects are very good, particularly cottonseed, sunflower seed and flaxseed, which are the most important.

Sugar production is estimated to be about 138,000 short tons,
slightly lower than last year, but with carry-over stocks, considered

to be sufficient to meet domestic requirements.

With the exception of citrus, which was damaged by frost, fresh fruits and vegetable crops are estimated to be about average. Raisins and figs were damaged by dry, hot weather which reduced quantities available for export.

The hazelnut crop was only about one-third of last year's. Resultant higher prices for export nuts may decrease local availability. However, the walnut crop, which is largely consumed domestically, was good.

The rains in the fall of 1950 have been most favorable for the sowing of grains. Cereal acreage will show a marked increase over last year, as a result of breaking up of new lands, the distribution of additional state lands to farmers and the increased use of tillage and seeding equipment financed by the Economic Cooperation Administration.

Production of edible pulses is reported to be about 20 percent higher than in 1949. Surpluses for export are estimated at 75,000 short tons compared with 53,000 short tons in 1949. In addition, stocks on hand from the 1949 crop are estimated at 22,000 short tons. In order to encourage the export of old stocks, the government has agreed to allow exporters the use of the foreign exchange to import any quantity of the goods appearing on the general import list.

Iran: In general, the production of food in 1950 has been much better than in 1949 with substantial surpluses in many items. This year's production of wheat was 20 percent larger than last year's, and there will be a considerable carry-over for the 1951-52 consumption year. About 50-60,000 short tons of barley will be available for export. Rice production in 1950 is estimated at 340,000 short tons (clean basis) compared with 285,000 short tons in 1949. About 75,000 short tons will be available for export.

Total production of pulses and vegetables is larger than last year. About 7,000 short tons of pulses will be available for export. As a result of good crops dried and fresh fruits are also in excess of local needs, and considerable amounts will be available for export.

Sugar production, estimated at 50,000 short tons, is 64 percent more than 1949. There was a carry-over from last year of about 55,000 short tons, making a total supply of over 100,000 short tons available for consumption during the 1950-51 season. Since domestic consumption is expected to amount to about 167,000 short tons, and since a carry-over at the end of the year of some 55,000 short tons is considered advisable, it should be necessary to import about 142,000 short tons before September, 1951.

Animal fats are seldom exported or imported, and local production is considered sufficient to meet the demand. The production of fats in 1950 was about 1,000 short tons greater than last year. Also the production of vegetable oils was 1,500 short tons higher. It is expected that about 1,500 short tons will be imported during 1951.

Meat and poultry production has been better than last year, due to better pastures and abundant feeds and will be sufficient to meet local needs.

The recent trade agreements between Iran, the Soviet Union, Germany and France will more than absorb all the available surpluses of dates, raisins, almonds, pistachio nuts, rice and dried apricots.

Egypt: The shortage of bread grains in 1950-51 is greater than usual. It has been increasing from year to year as a result of population growth. The deficit of wheat and corn this year is estimated at about 780,000 short tons. It must be met through imports, partly under the terms of the International Wheat Agreement, and partly through bilateral trade agreements. At the end of 1950, imports and closed purchases amounted to about 500,000 short tons, and the remainder is expected to be secured before the summer harvest of 1951. The 130,000 short tons of corn promised by Yugoslavia in exchange for Egyptian cotton will not be forthcoming due to the serious Yugoslavian drought. About 110,000 short tons of wheat have been supplied by the Soviet Union in exchange for cotton. Substantial shipments are expected also from Canada, Australia and the United States.

Sugar production was below normal, due to smaller acreage and lower yields in 1949-50. The deficit was met through imports. Normal production is expected in 1950-51, but it is likely to fall short of the increasing demand.

Cottonseed oil is another important item in Egyptian diet. Local production in 1950, as in 1949, was sufficient to meet the country's needs. If the officially decreed restriction on cotton acreage in 1951 is actually put into effect, it may create a deficit which could be met by imports of cottonseed from the Sudan.

Egypt has an exportable surplus of about 350,000 short tons of cleaned rice and 100,000 short tons of onions.

The major features of Egyptian food policy for 1951 may be summarized as follows: (1) Reduction of the cotton acreage, in favor of food crops. (2) Maintenance of a surplus rice production. (3) Exchange of cotton and rice for imports of bread grains, especially wheat.

Syria: As a result of favorable weather conditions and increased acreages, Syrian crop production was excellent, with wheat setting an all-time record. Thus the exportable surpluses of bread grains are estimated at 340,000 short tons. Large shipments have already been made to neighboring countries.

Because of an unusually severe winter, olive trees suffered serious damage, and the olive oil crop was short. Consequently, there will not be the usual exportable surplus, but enough to satisfy local consumption.

The principal food imports will consist, as usual, of about 30,000 short tons of sugar and some 5,000 short tons of rice.

Lebanon: Lebanon is a deficit producer of the staple food items; but import requirements for the 1950-51 season of some 150,000 short tons of grains will be provided mainly by Syria, and livestock for slaughter, mainly sheep, by Turkey and Iraq. The main food surpluses are expected to consist of some 12,000 short tons of deciduous fruit, 15,000 short tons of citrus and 65,000 short tons of vegetables.

Israel: Israel is a deficit producer of foodstuffs, and has to depend upon imports for the major portion of the staple items. This deficit has been increasing, with the rapid increase in population resulting from intensive immigration. The citrus crop, the main export item of the country, has not yet recovered from the damage it suffered in the war between Israel and the Arab States two years ago. Furthermore, producers are finding it difficult to compete with the Spanish and other crops in European markets.

Despite successful effort by the Government to increase food production, Israel again must depend heavily upon imports of bread grains, rice, sugar, livestock and products, and other food items.

Iraq: For the second consecutive year, favorable weather and ample irrigation water resulted in record crops in Iraq during the summer and fall of 1950. Consequently, the country is in a position to meet all of its grain requirements for 1951, and also offer for export surpluses of about 200,000 short tons of wheat, 600,000 short tons of barley and 50,000 short tons of rice. A very good date crop was harvested also in the fall of 1950, with an exportable surplus estimated at 250,000 short tons. Livestock, an important source of food in Iraq, is reported to have entered the winter season in good condition. Normally, about 200,000 head (mostly sheep) are exported annually to neighboring countries.

THE FAR EAST

The 1951 food supply outlook in the Far East appears to be slightly
better than that which prevailed during 1950. This is the case despite
the fact that military activities are likely to affect adversely the
distribution of foodstuffs over large areas both of Northeast and Southeast Asia, and that India in 1950 apparently experienced a crop year
complicated by droughts, floods and insect pests.

With the exception of India, crops generally were good in Far Eastern
countries in 1950. Indian production of foodgrains was reduced about
7 percent below last year by a variety of natural calamities that
affected practically the entire·Indian Union. India is normally only
90 percent self-sufficient in foodstuffs and in 1951 its dependence
upon food imports will be increased. Pakistan's total production of
food in 1950 approximated 1949 levels. There will no doubt be some
exports of wheat, rice and minor grains in 1951, but the amount of
such exports is uncertain. The situation in Ceylon appears favorable,
largely due to the fact that high prices for its principal exports
(rubber, tea, coconuts) assures it of an adequate supply of foreign
exchange with which to purchase food abroad if imports are available.

There may be slightly larger rice exports from Asia's traditionally
surplus rice-producing countries -- Burma, Thailand and Indochina --
but any increase is contingent upon an improvement in the internal
situation in Burma and Indochina, where civil dissension has disrupted
the production and distribution of foodstuffs. Thailand is the only
one of the three countries to equal prewar levels in rice production,
but none is expected to suffer from food shortages.

Malaya, like Ceylon, depends heavily upon imported food, particularly
rice. However, its large exports of rubber and tin at high prices
places it in a favorable procurement position wherever rice is available. In the Republic of Indonesia the food supply appears secure
until the April harvest, despite a slightly smaller rice crop. Total
crop production in 1950 approximated 1949 levels. The levels of food
consumption vary greatly between regions, however, and the large
number of widely scattered islands in the Republic makes anything but
a generalized statement concerning the food situation there impossible.

In the Philippines the 1950 rice crop set a record and the food supply
for 1951 appears assured. Other crops were also good and despite
gains in population, which tend to cancel out increases in food
production, it seems that the 1951 per capita consumption of staple
foods other than rice will approximate the prewar level.

The improved food situation in Japan is due to good crops and an
acceleration in foreign trade. Japan depends heavily upon Southeast
Asia for its rice supplies and increased exports to that area of
cotton textiles and machinery has made it possible for the country
to pay for an increased proportion of its rice imports from earned

foreign exchange. Per capita consumption of food in Japan is now about 95 percent of prewar.

Four years of continued improvement in the domestic food supply of the Repuolic of Korea came to an abrupt halt with the Communist invasion in June. Although a good 1950 rice crop was harvested with little damage from military activity the food supply situation for 1951 is highly precarious. The inadequate transportation and distribution system has been completely disrupted by war. Imports of fertilizer have been superseded by the need for military supplies. Only an early end to the armed conflict will prevent extreme hunger and starvation among Korea's millions of refugees.

The food situation in China and Manchuria appears better than a year ago but available data on crop production are insufficient for an acceptable statistical analysis. Unusually favorable production figures issued by the Chinese Communist regime do not appear reasonable in the light of the available cultivated area, scarcity of seeds due to the poor 1949 crops, and other factors. The extent to which the political aims of the Peiping regime will result in continued military activity will have a direct bearing on the food situation in China during 1951. In 1951, as last year, surplus food in Manchuria appears destined for the Soviet Union. Formosa has a large domestic supply of food, with both sugar and rice available for export.

India

Foodgrain production in India will be dangerously low in 1950-51 and the total indigenous food supply is likely to be the smallest in years. In recent years India has produced about 45 million tons of foodgrains annually. This year production may fall to 42.6 million tons, a reduction of 7 percent. India's food problem is chronic, and is rooted in the static pattern of primitive production practices. Crop yields per acre are low due to lack of knowledge, incentive and material means. These basic factors have been aggravated in 1950-51 by floods and drought which have seriously reduced rice crop prospects, possibly by as much as 2 million tons. There is little probability that this loss will be offset to any important extent by larger production of wheat, barley and gram this winter.

The critical food situation in India was alleviated somewhat in late 1950 by the arrival of milo, part of a total of 427,000 tons made available to India by the United States Government.

Foodgrains normally constitute about 20 percent of India's total imports. India's dependence upon imports will be greater in 1951. It started the year with dangerously low stocks on hand. Local procurement of rice, which ranged from 100,000 to 150,000 tons per week from the end of 1949 to the spring of 1950, will be smaller this year because of a decrease in production of rice in part of the principal

rice-producing States. The quantity of wheat to be procured during the
spring and early summer months cannot be foreseen at this time, but it
is not likely to be more than last year. On the other hand, the off-
take of foodgrains for rationing purposes may be expected to increase
above the rate of 140,000 to 150,000 tons per week because of the
necessity of distributing more foodgrains in drought-stricken rural
areas.

The Indian Government assumes the responsibility of collecting grain
from surplus regions for rationing in deficit areas. Government
stocks of foodgrain have been dwindling rapidly. Officials had
hoped to reduce ration requirements in 1950 to 6.5 million tons and
to supply all but 1.5 million tons from domestic procurement. However,
only 4.6 million tons were procured locally, imports were much less
than in 1949, ration requirements have continued at the 8 million ton
rate, and emergency demands have been increasing. Diversion of
acreage to non-food crops may reduce foodgrain production slightly.
In some areas the daily foodgrain ration has been reduced from 12 to
9 ounces per person.

Cereals comprise the major part of the Indian diet and rice a greater
part than all other grains combined. Meats, eggs and dairy products
are usually of negligible quantity and there is no indication that
any significant change will occur in the consumption level of non-
cereal foods in 1951.

Pakistan

Pakistan generally is self-sufficient in food supplies and in addition
has a small amount of foodgrains available for export. Wheat is the
principal grain produced in West Pakistan, while rice is the main crop
and food item in East Pakistan.

The supply of domestic wheat that will be available from the 1950-51
crop is estimated to be only slightly lower than last year, despite
September floods in the Punjab. The floods occurred before the wheat
crop was planted so that the damage was confined largely to stocks in
storage. Estimates indicate that jowar (grain sorghums) production may
have been reduced by at least 10 percent. Exports of grain were suspended
in October until the exact damage of the Punjab floods could be
determined. Exports may be resumed soon but since the wheat crop
harvest will not be completed until some time in April, the magnitude
of such exports will not be known for some time.

East Pakistan wavers on the brink of self-sufficiency as far as the
production of rice is concerned. The 1950-51 crop will probably be a
little larger than the previous year's, and about 13 percent above
the prewar average. Last year Pakistan exported some rice and expects
to export a small amount again this year. There is some indication
that the pressure on food supplies in East Pakistan may have been
alleviated somewhat by the migration of many rice-eating Hindus to

India, thus leaving a small surplus for shipment to countries outside
of Pakistan.

The production of millets, corn and barley, as a group, are expected
to be slightly less than for the year before, but small exports will
probably be made during the remainder of this fiscal year ending
next March 31.

Pakistan continues to be short of refined sugar and may import as
much as 100,000 tons in 1951. Vegetable oils are also in short supply,
particularly mustard, rapeseed and coconut oils. These will be imported
in undetermined quantities from Ceylon, Malaya and India.

Ceylon

The average Ceylonese depends principally on rice as the mainstay of his
diet. Diets also include pulses, green leaves and dried fish, as well
as locally-grown fruits and vegetables such as pineapples, mangoes,
pawpaws, gourds, cabbage and turnips. There is a high level of sugar
consumption, the daily average being about 1.6 ounces per person.

Rice production in Ceylon is only about 40 percent of domestic requirements. While rubber, tea and coconuts are profitable crops, they also
increase the pressure on food supplies and Ceylon must import 60 percent of her food requirements. Food imports comprise about 50 percent
of all imports, at a total cost equal to one-quarter of the national
income. Ceylon's population is increasing rapidly and the Government
is interested in reducing the country's growing dependence upon food
imports. It has embarked on a program of purchasing marginal rubber
lands for conversion into food producing acreage. This program is
progressing slowly, however, because of the current high price of
rubber.

An average rice crop is in prospect for 1950-51. It will probably be
13 percent smaller than last year's crop but about 17 percent larger
than prewar. Imports of rice, mostly from Burma, were about 300,000
short tons during the first-half of 1950, above the rate for the same
period in 1949. Imports of rice and other foodstuffs will continue
to be large in 1951, but due to the favorable prices prevailing for
Ceylon's principal export products, the Ceylonese will have no
difficulty if the required supplies are available.

Burma, Thailand (Siam) and Indochina

This area is the world's great rice surplus region, exporting 6.3 million
short tons annually before the war, or 63 percent of the world's rice
exports and 68 percent of those of Asia. Since World War II only Thailand has managed to increase its acreage and production to the prewar
level. Total exports of these countries in 1950 came to 2.8 million
short tons, roughly 45 percent of the prewar average. Slight increases
in exports tentatively are expected during 1951 but will be contingent

in large part upon improvement in Burma's internal situation and Vietnam's (Eastern Indochina) economic policy and military conditions.

In addition to rice, Burma, Thailand and Indochina grow a variety of other crops in such abundance that widespread food shortages are a remote hazard. Such crops include corn, pulses, oilseeds, vegetables and fruit, some of which normally are exported. Fish is an important protein component in the diet, while meat is eaten to a lesser extent.

Burma: The rice harvested beginning at the close of 1950 for consumption and export in 1951 approximated the previous harvest in both acreage and production; an estimated 9.2 million acres produced about 4.0 million short tons. This was around 73 percent of average prewar production. Exports during 1950 came to 1.3 million tons, roughly equal to those of 1949 and about 40 percent of the prewar level. Exports in 1951 are expected to approximate those of the two preceding years.

The military situation improved during 1950 but not in time to benefit either the rice crop then growing or 1951 exports. Should conditions continue to improve, it is anticipated that the harvest starting in December of 1951 will be larger and 1952 exports appreciably greater.

Thailand (Siam): Thailand's rice production increased from an average of 3.4 million short tons before the war to 3.9 million in 1948-49 and to 4.1 in both 1949-50 and 1950-51, an increase of 23 percent over prewar. Recent increases in rice production have been more than offset by the food requirements of an expanded population so that, while exports in 1949 approximated the prewar average, 1.5 million short tons, 1951 exports are expected to be about the same or nearly as large as the prewar average.

Indochina: Adverse political and military conditions in Indochina continue to depress rice production and limit exports to a fraction of the prewar level. The 1949-50 crop produced 4.3 million short tons and the harvest recently completed for 1951 consumption is estimated at 3.9 million tons, 78 percent of average prewar production. Stocks of rice within Indochina were adequate for domestic needs but civil strife and attendant transportation difficulties led to temporary shortages in some areas, notably in the more highly industrialized north.

Exports in 1950 came to 90,000 short tons, only 6 percent of prewar. The decline in exports is due in large part to the Government's blockade of the rebel-dominated surplus areas in the south. The area accounted for a great part of Indochinese exports which are not likely to increase significantly until the blockade is lifted. Also, a recent edict intended to protect local supplies forbids exports to countries outside the French Union and limits shipments within it. In brief, rice exports from Indochina are for the most part contingent upon political and military conditions. No significant increases in exports during 1951 are expected.

Malaya

The food outlook for Malaya for 1951 is reasonably good. The 1949-50
rice crop is estimated at 496,000 short tons of milled rice, 133,000
tons above the crop recorded for 1948-49. This large crop is attributed
to favorable weather conditions. The area planted for the 1950-51
crop is estimated at 930,000 acres, approximately the same as for the
1949-50 crop. Rice production for 1950-51 is estimated at 418,000
short tons of milled rice, or about 10 percent below last year's crop.

Total availability of rice for Malaya, including Singapore, for the
year 1950 is estimated at 1 million short tons, excluding inventory
changes, of which 477,000 tons are from domestic production and 523,000
tons from net imports. This availability averages about 14.6 ounces
per capita per day. This contrasts with a reported per capita daily
consumption of 17.3 ounces for the prewar years of 1934-38.

Rice import requirements for 1951 are estimated at 560,000 short tons.
Malaya's current large exports of rubber and tin at high prices places
her in a favorable position to procure rice if the supply is available.

During 1948 and 1949 Malaya consumed about 112,000 short tons of wheat
flour annually, all of which was imported. It is estimated that Malaya
will have a wheat flour import requirement in 1951 of at least 112,000
short tons.

Indonesia

The food situation in the Republic of Indonesia remains less satisfactory
than before World War II as a result of unsettled economic and political
conditions. The consumption level for the current year in Java and
Madura will be considerably lower than the prewar average of 1,982
calories.

Rice acreage and production in 1950 appeared to be about 9.8 million
acres and 5 million short tons (milled) or slightly below prewar levels.
The rice crop planted early in 1951 is expected to approximate that of
1950. Following years of declining imports, Indonesia became a net
exporter of rice for the first time in 1941. Since the war, however,
greater food requirements stemming from subsequent population growth
have caused imports to increase. Internal difficulties impeded
distribution of rice stocks throughout the islands so that rice
shortages occurred in some places during 1950. Imports of about
300,000 tons will be required during 1951.

As a result of lowered per capita rice supplies, production of sweet
potatoes, cassava and sago has increased in recent years, although only
fruits, vegetables, soybeans and coconut products are eaten in quantities
comparable to prewar. Except for peanuts, per capita consumption of
other important foods has declined. The consumption of wheat flour,
which is wholly imported, declined from a prewar average of 115,000
short tons a year to 82,000 in the year ending June 1950.

Greater crop yields per acre can substantially increase food production on the main islands of Java and Madura, which are among the most heavily populated regions in the world. Their cultivated area is not likely to expand significantly, however. On the other hand, successful colonization of the lightly populated Outer Islands (Sumatra, Borneo, etc.), a project that is now underway, can add greatly to Indonesia's agricultural resources and improve its long-term food position.

Philippines

Food conditions during 1951 promise to be the best in the postwar period. Despite floods, coupled with continued political uprisings in the major rice-producing areas of Central Luzon, the rice crop harvested at the close of 1950 for consumption in 1951 established an all-time record. An estimated 5.7 million acres produced about 3 million short tons of rough rice, an increase over the average prewar acreage and production of 16 and 21 percent, respectively, and of 4 and 5 percent over the previous crop. Due to large stock carryovers from 1949, rice imports in 1950 were the smallest since the war. The retail price of rice was lower and more stable than in any other postwar period, although it was still far above the prewar level.

On the other hand, growth in the population of the Philippines and increases in consumption requirements have outpaced increases in rice output. Although production and imports since 1948 have been above the prewar rate, per capita rice supplies are still below the prewar level. In 1950 the annual per capita rice supply was estimated at 170 pounds as compared to 165 pounds in 1949 and 195 pounds in 1939. Philippine rice production is capable of expansion even greater than that recently registered. For the next few years, however, imports will continue to be needed to meet consumption requirements.

The supply of staple foods other than rice has been steadily improving. Corn production has expanded considerably during the past decade and it is believed that consumption during 1951 will approximate the prewar figure of about 60 pounds per person. Supplies of pulses and vegetables exceed prewar levels and will adequately fill the demand for them during the current year. Root crops, notably sweet potatoes, along with coconut oil and sugar will continue to be abundant. The International Wheat Agreement assures the Philippines a generally adequate supply of wheat and wheat flour.

The per capita consumption of fish is now greater than before the war, compensating for a decline in meat supplies. Fruits are now consumed in near normal quantities.

Japan

The food situation improved considerably during 1950 and Japan is showing a greater capacity to feed herself from her own economic resources. The consumption level was increased from 2,050 calories in 1950 to 2,100 calories for 1951, while the projected level for 1952 is 2,150 calories, 96 percent of prewar.

Staple food production in 1950 was the highest on record, amounting to slightly less than 15.2 million short tons in terms of milled rice equivalents, or roughly 2 percent more than either 1939 or 1948 production. The 1950 rice crop, estimated at 9.0 million short tons milled, was the second largest in the postwar period and 3 percent higher than the prewar average. The sweet potato acreage declined in 1950 but high yields increased total production to 6.9 million short tons, 6 percent above the previous harvest. The production of other staples, wheat, barley and minor cereals, compared favorably with preceding years.

The staple food collections proceeded satisfactorily, although rice collections in the fall of 1950 came in more slowly than in 1949. The 1949-50 collection quota was exceeded, providing about 7.1 million short tons of milled rice and assuring the urban areas adequate supplies.

Increased imports were noted during the fiscal year ending June 30, 1950, totaling over 4.2 million short tons, while slightly higher imports are expected during the current fiscal year. Rice imports during fiscal year 1951 are expected to total 770,000 short tons, as compared to 660,000 tons in the preceding year and an average of about 2.2 million tons prewar. During late 1950 soybean imports from Communist China were cut off and procurement of soybeans in the United States was difficult, and may result in curtailed consumption of the important protein foods, miso (soy paste) and shoyu (soy sauce). Peanuts and other foods normally imported from China will be similarly affected.

A significant development during 1950 was the substantial rise in the proportion of total food imports financed from Japanese resources. During 1951 purchases from Japanese funds will cover 70 percent of total imports while GARIOA (occupation) funds will account for 30 percent.

Controls were removed from potatoes in January 1950, but are retained on the other important staples, rice, wheat and barley. Otherwise the trend has been toward decontrolling commodities as they become more plentiful. Fats and oils have been decontrolled, as has sugar, although the latter is still distributed through official channels. Supplies of fresh fruits, vegetables and fish have been and are expected to remain adequate. As the staple food situation improved during 1950 and black-market prices continued to decline, consumers became increasingly quality-conscious and began to reject the less desirable foods offered as part of the staple ration, notably processed potato products and coarse grains. During the past year, however, substantial increases were noted in the overall price of food.

In general, it may be stated that Japanese food production is near its maximum level and, while slight increases can be expected in the future,

these will be more than offset by population increases. The increased
production of the past year tends to offset the food deficit arising
from population growth, however, so that the increase in food imports
during 1951 reflects greater economic prosperity. It appears
inevitable, though, that the Japanese deficit in cereals, sugar and
soybeans will increase as years go by.

Republic of Korea

Since the Communist invasion of South Korea on June 25, 1950, military
operations have so disrupted the activities of the Ministry of Agriculture and Forestry that the crop reporting and food distribution
systems have largely ceased to function. Nevertheless, the Ministry
has made estimates of acreages planted and yields for 1950. These
estimates are probably low in view of the heavy application of
fertilizer to the 1950 crop and relatively insignificant damage to
the crop by military operations.

Total availabilities of food in 1951 from the 1950-51 crop, from sea
fishing and from farm slaughter of livestock plus eggs and milk are
likely to be somewhat less than in 1950. The 1950 rice crop is
estimated at 2,392,000 short tons of milled rice, 130,000 tons less
than the 1949 crop. The 1951 crop of summer foodgrains is likely to
be substantially less than the 1,072,000 short tons (polished rice
equivalents) harvested in 1950. This will come about because of
reduced plantings of fall grains occasioned by the general state of
insecurity everywhere across the peninsula and from the lack of
commercial fertilizer. So far as can be foreseen, practically no
commercial fertilizer will be available for application on 1950-51
crops in South Korea, except for the small carry-over in the fall
of 1950.

From the 1949 rice crop a net export of 88,000 short tons milled was
made to Japan. Because of the disruption and heavy damage to trans-
port and distribution facilities it became necessary to bring in
foodgrains from outside sources in the late fall of 1950.

The food situation in South Korea had been improving each year
beginning with 1946. Large amounts of imported fertilizer made
possible the increased production of foodgrains. Supplies of ocean-
caught fish remained relatively constant at about 330,000 short tons
annually. However, the per capita consumption of fish was less
because of the great influx of refugees from North Korea and the
repatriation of Korean nationals from adjacent areas. The damage
to and destruction and confiscation of fishing vessels in South Korea
during the present war has been very considerable. The lack of
petroleum and fishing gear and supplies for the fishing fleet are
likely further to reduce the fish-catch in 1951, thereby adversely
affecting the food supply.

It has been reported that undetermined but very considerable losses
of livestock -- work cattle, hogs and chickens -- occurred in July
and August 1950 as the Communist hordes moved south across the
peninsula. Apart from the effects of these losses upon the protein
component in the Korean diet, large losses of work stock will
seriously retard the preparation of land for foodgrain plantings.

It is probable that a shortage of foodgrains will occur in 1951
beginning in May or June and lasting until October when the 1951 rice
harvest will begin. Taking account of imports made in the closing
months of 1950, the foodgrain deficit in 1951 is likely to be on the
order of 330,000 short tons. If deaths attributable directly to the
ravages of war exceed substantially the normal net annual excess of
births over deaths of 350,000, the foodgrain deficit may be largely
reduced if not entirely eliminated.

China

A year ago China was enduring widespread hunger and privation as a
result of floods, droughts and other natural calamities throughout
the country. Food production in 1949 was 10 percent lower than both
1948 production and the 1931-37 average. The food situation is
generally believed to be slightly improved this year due to better
growing conditions in 1950, although reliable statistics on production
of the various crops are non-existent. The food situation in 1951,
however, will no doubt be serious in many parts of the country due to
poor transportation facilities, the stagnation of economic life, growing
discontent among the population and dislocations caused by the operations
of the Chinese Communist army.

The controlled press of Communist China has steadfastly maintained
that the 1950 crops were close to a record. Wheat production has been
stated as being 20 percent larger than the 1949 crop, from an acreage
estimated as only 9 percent larger. This appears to be an exaggerated
estimate as an abrupt increase of this size seems quite impossible
under the unfavorable production environment which prevailed,
notably the acute shortage of seeds, due to poor harvest in 1949, and
general confusion caused by the impact of Communist "land reform" and
postwar economic and social dislocations. With regard to acreage, a
2 to 3 percent increase over 1949 would seem reasonable on the basis
of extensive reclamation and water conservancy undertakings.

No figures are available on the total production of rice, but unusually
favorable Communist estimates claim better than average production of
paddy in Hupeh, Fukien, Kwangsi and Kiangsi Provinces.

Despite the predominantly agricultural character of her economy, China
normally is a net importer of foodstuffs. Before the Communists
conquered the country annual food imports were in the neighborhood of
1.7 million short tons. Since 1949 China's normal channels of trade
have been disrupted so that no reliable information on Chinese food
imports are available.

Manchuria

According to the New China (Communist) News Agency, grain production
in the Northeast (Manchuria plus part of Jehol) in 1950 totalled
19,958,000 short tons, or 37 percent over 1949 production. Acreage
planted last year was estimated as being 3.8 percent greater than the
38.5 million acres planted in 1949. Yield per acre is stated as
exceeding the record under the Japanese occupation period by 6 percent.
The area under soybeans in 1950 was 22 percent larger than in 1949.
Wheat and rice also topped the pre-Sino-Japanese War record.

The above estimates of production are difficult to reconcile with
production statistics for previous years because of Communist-made
changes in the administrative regions of China and Manchuria. The
region commonly known as Manchuria is referred to by the Communist
regime as the Northeast and now includes a part of Jehol Province as
well. However, the estimated big increase of 1950 grain production
over the previous year seems incompatible with the very modest
increase of acreage for the same period. Factors such as good weather,
strengthening and broadening of the mutual-aid labor system and improvement in farming techniques pointed out by the Communists can hardly
justify such a large increase. While 1950 production was probably
higher than the low of 1949, problems such as shortage of seeds,
fertilizers and rural capital would seem to have prevented such an
effective utilization of land resources as claimed.

Manchuria is normally a food surplus area and in prewar years it
exported about 2.7 million short tons of foodstuffs annually. There
will undoubtedly be some exports of foodgrains, particularly soybeans,
during 1951 but these exports will probably go in the main to the
Soviet Union. The ban imposed on trade with China by the United
States and other Western nations will probably restrict the legal
movement of foodstuffs to countries other than the Soviet Union.

Formosa (Taiwan)

Favorable weather, a plentiful supply of fertilizer and a reasonably
stable politico-economic situation in Formosa have combined to create
the most favorable food situation in many years. The 1950 record rice
crop of 1.4 million short tons of milled rice is about 4 percent above
prewar and assures an exportable surplus, despite the fact that
domestic consumption of rice has about doubled while the population
has increased only 50 percent. The average Formosan consumes about
20 ounces of rice per day compared to the Indian ration of 12 ounces
of foodgrains per day. Some difficulty has been experienced in getting
the Formosan rice on the market because of the low prices paid to the farmer.

Formosa had a bumper peanut crop and good crops of fruits and vegetables.
The production of sugar is still far below the prewar output. Production
of raw sugar in 1950 is estimated at 450,000 short tons, compared to
the prewar average of 1,202,000 tons. The decrease in production is
due largely to the prevailing low price of sugar.

CENTRAL AFRICA

The food situation for 1950-51 in Central Africa was improved by
late 1950 seasonal rains and was reported better than normal in most
producing areas. British East Africa generally enjoyed bumper crops,
although there were crop failures in large-scale enterprises in oilseeds
and nuts. In British West Africa and French Equatorial Africa, drought
caused some shortages, particularly in grainstuffs, while palm and seed
oils and cocoa showed increases. The drought adversely affected livestock
production and most crops in Southern Rhodesia. Production of food
crops in Angola was exceptionally good in 1950; however, shortages were
reported in meat. The Congo continued to increase its production of
palm oil.

An unusually menacing locust infestation spreading from the Red
Sea countries into British East Africa and surrounding areas has caused
widespread control measures to be instituted, particularly in Kenya.
Damage due to "leaf rust" disease in the Gold Coast necessitated imports
of rice and corn. A more general complaint, however, was lack of farm
labor.

In an effort to counteract the trend toward over-emphasis on production of export crops, governments in Africa are generally giving added
attention to measures to increase production of food for local consumption.
It is officially reported from Southern Rhodesia, for example, that there
is no self-sufficiency in any single food crop. Measures to increase
production of food for consumption have included land settlement and
large-scale production schemes, mechanization, use of fertilizers, irrigation, export control measures, and educational programs. The construc-
tion of storage, refrigeration, and food-processing facilities is a
factor in the improved food situation, particularly in regard to vegetable
oils in several areas in Africa.

Government and corporate food production schemes are expected to
bring several vast tracts into cultivation in 1951 and 1952, particularly
in Nigeria, despite crop failures in the British-sponsored peanut scheme
and abandonment of considerable acreage in Tanganyika.

Complete recovery from the 1949 production slump in the East African
food position was shown in the bumper corn and wheat harvests in Nyanza
Province. It is estimated that a combined corn and wheat surplus of
approximately 65,000 short tons will be exported in the next few months,
chiefly to Western Germany. Rainfall during the second quarter was
below normal in some grazing areas. The livestock industry benefited,
however, from higher local market prices.

East African agriculture found relief during the year through
increased local and export prices. Dairy and cattle prices were revised
upwards, as were grains, feeds, rice, and tobacco. Growers of the main
cash and export crops, that is, sisal, coffee, cotton, cloves, and tea,
were experiencing a profitable year from high world market prices.
Concerted action by Kenya coffee growers resulted in more favorable

contract terms with the British Ministry of Food.

The area under palm cultivation in the Belgian Congo is expanding and production of palm oil is increasing by about 5,500 short tons a year. Local consumption of oilseed cakes by livestock (chiefly in the eastern part of the Congo) increased by about 50 percent in 1950 and a further increase is expected in 1951 as part of a campaign to increase locally-produced meat supplies.

Increased yields in coffee from new plantings after World War II were first realized in 1950 in the Congo and Ruandi-Urundi. Due to the time required for processing and transporting, the yields will show up in exports for 1951. The revised forecast for the 1950-51 crop year total production is 550,000 sacks, 540,000 of which are for export.

Cultivation of corn, the only important grain export, is increasing in the Congo. Consumption of wheat flour, chiefly from the United States, is steadily increasing. Manioc, the most important cultivated crop, is mainly locally consumed. Production of manioc for 1950 is estimated to be slightly higher than 1949.

In Nigeria, a shortage in foodstuffs, acute by autumn of 1950, was accompanied by rising prices of foodstuffs and demands for increased wages. The increasing inflationary pressure caused initially by the effects of devaluation (in the Fall of 1949) was given added impetus by the Korean conflict.

Rains during the early growing season in Nigeria were light, causing all crops to be late. This dry period was followed in the North by abnormally heavy rains, so that the agricultural production exceeded early expectations. 1950-51 crops for export were estimated at from 253-275,000 short tons, which about equals the 10-year average but is considerably below the crop exports of the past 4 years, which were about 300,000 long tons.

Rice production in Nigeria is expected to increase slowly, owing to the shortage of food. It is estimated that about 125,000 acres of rice are under cultivation. Informed sources have predicted fair to good exportable crop of about 110,000 tons of cocoa for the 1950-51 buying season, which opened September 22, in Nigeria.

British West Africa normally exports each year 1,000,000 tons of peanuts, sesame seed, palm kernels, palm oil and cotton seed. The return from nuts and oilseeds shipped to the United Kingdom in 1951 is expected to be one-fourth to one-third percent more than in 1950.

In French Equatorial Africa production of vegetable oil is expected to expand in 1951. Three oil mills are being placed in operation for processing cotton seeds and peanuts. The improvements in processing of oils, being made in Africa, have made available a residue of sufficiently low oil content to render it palatable to livestock and thus boost meat production.

In French West Africa cocoa production is expected to be about 55,000 to 60,000 short tons for 1950-51, compared to a production of slightly over 60,000 short tons in 1949-50, and about 55,000 tons in 1948-49.

The exportable surplus of coffee from French West Africa for 1950-51 is forecast at 48,000 to 50,000 tons, which is about the average for the two preceding years.

Production of vegetable oils is scheduled for a sharp increase, due to large-scale agricultural operations, principally in peanuts. The 1950 peanut crop was first to be harvested in this program and the number of acres cultivated was 1,482 acres, compared with 4,681 for 1951. A total of 74,100 acres are due to be cleared for planting by 1955.

French Equatorial Africa shows an increase in livestock over preceding years. The number of cattle listed for 1950 was 1,427,000, as compared with 1,418,000 for 1948 and 1,314,000 for 1946. For sheep-goats the figures show for 1950, 1,540,000, as compared to 1,258,000 for 1949 and 1,042,000 for 1948.

Imports of flour are expected to increase steadily. The percentage supplied by the United States, the main source of flour, is declining and the percentage of imports from France is increasing.

Coffee, Angola's most important crop, was harvested from May to August 1950, and was exceptionally good. Late 1950 estimates place production for export at 840,000 (132.3 lb.) bags, as compared with 520,000 bags in 1949, and a 1935-39 average exportable production of only 275,000 bags annually.

Bean production in Angola in the past two years has increased sharply over previous years. The 1950 crop was estimated at 1,200,000 bags of 100 pounds as compared with 1,323,000 in 1949, and a 1940-44 average of 646,000 bags.

During 1950 there was a severe meat shortage in northern Angola and in the latter part of the year it spread to other areas. Distortions in the controlled price structure are considered to have been a major factor in this shortage, which is said to be a relatively new development in the Colony's food supply situation.

In Liberia production of food crops, principally rice, cassava, and vegetables, was considerably below 1949 levels because of army worms and drought conditions. On the other hand, meat, poultry, and fish production are at the highest level since the establishment of the Liberian Department of Agriculture and Commerce in 1947.

The Liberian Government has encouraged the planting of supplemental food crops to offset the shortages, and additional lands were prepared for cultivation.

UNION OF SOUTH AFRICA

The corn crop harvested in 1950 was larger than average and enough to supply the demand for both human consumption and for livestock feed. Other cereal crops, however, were below normal, including oats, rye, barley and wheat. The rainfall during November was unfavorable for planting of corn. Consequently, the 1951 crop is forecast at slightly less than normal domestic consumption requirements. A larger-than-normal quantity of wheat was imported during 1949-50, but prospects for 1950-51 are for a normal to slightly above normal wheat crop.

Meat supplies are short and the outlook is for a continued short supply during 1951. While pork has been in adequate supply, beef has been less than sufficient to meet demand, and mutton has been in extremely short supply. Poultry production has been sufficient to supply the demand. The production of dairy products has increased, and import requirements of condensed milk reduced.

The canned vegetable industry is producing increased quantities for export, particularly to other areas in Africa. Prospects generally appear favorable for increased exportable surpluses of canned fruit, fruit juices and fresh citrus fruit.

AUSTRALIA AND NEW ZEALAND

Australia and New Zealand, during 1950, continued to be among the best
fed nations in the world. Ample amounts of all essential foods, with a
few temporary exceptions, were available to satisfy domestic demand. The
principal exports of foodstuffs, including meats and dairy products, were
maintained at a high level during 1949-50. New developments in 1950-51
are expected to be some decline in Australia's exportable surplus of
wheat, and a significant increase in the sheep population of both countries.

The 1949-50 Australian wheat harvest was large. The crop amounted to
215 million bushels, of which 115 million were exported. Another large
crop was expected in 1950-51, but prolonged rains during October and
November reduced its size and, to some extent, its quality. Consequently,
a national crop of average size, perhaps in the neighborhood of 185 million
bushels, instead of the 200 million bushels prophesied, was being harvested at the end of the calendar year 1950. Exports of wheat for 1950-51,
according to current estimates, may not be more than 85 million bushels.
Larger-than-average quantities of wheat probably will be fed to livestock
in New South Wales and Queensland as a result of the adverse effect of
the weather on its millability.

In both Australia and New Zealand, cattle and sheep numbers are larger
than a year ago and domestic meat consumption is expected to continue at
a high level. The overall domestic production and consumption of milk
and milk products was higher in 1949-50 than in 1948-49. Butter rationing was terminated in Australia on June 16, 1950. A leveling off of meat
and cheese exports and a significant rise in condensed as well as dried
milk exports is taking place. Exports of meat, cheese and butter continue
to be shipped largely to the United Kingdom under long-term contracts.
A program for disposing of some of these products elsewhere has produced
some sales outside Britain, including small shipments of lamb and of
cheese to the United States during the last fiscal year. Dried and condensed milk exports are going to a growing number and widely distributed
group of countries.

CANADA

Though adverse weather reduced both the yield and the quality of the
wheat crop, and of some fruit crops, there was, on the whole, a satisfactory Canadian food and feed output in 1950. Domestic food consumption
continued, showing some increase in the case of meat, milk, eggs and
poultry, and resulting in reduced exports of some commodities. Exports
of live cattle to the United States continued large but the marketings
of livestock products to the United Kingdom were considerably curtailed.
Surpluses or carry-over stocks of exportable foodstuffs at the end of
1950, were much below those on hand at the beginning of the year. The
generally high level of employment and wages is such that a high level
of domestic food consumption will continue during 1951.

Despite severe frost in August and bad harvesting weather in Western
Canada, wheat production for 1950 was higher than for 1949, and also
above the 10-year average. The available supply of wheat, including
the carry-over from the 1949 crop and the estimated 1950 output, will
permit increased domestic consumption and provide an exportable surplus
of 275 million bushels, compared with 225 million bushels for the previous year. As a result of the weather, damage to the 1950 wheat crop
will not average as high a grade as in previous years. Large feedgrain
supplies, including feed-grade wheat, will favor increased feeding of
livestock during the crop year 1950-51.

Overall Canadian meat production showed a rise of 6 percent for the
12 months ending September 30, 1950, compared with the previous 12
months. A trend towards lower volume has been noted in marketings of
cattle, calves, sheep and lambs. A downward trend was also indicated
in lower hog marketings in the last calendar quarter of 1950. However,
it is anticipated that the favorable feed situation may stimulate
breeding so that marketings of hogs will increase towards the end of
1951.

Little change in total milk production took place in 1950, but there was
a shift in utilization. There was increased consumption of fluid milk,
butter, and cream, and increased utilization of milk by the concentrated
milk industry. There was, however, a decline in utilization of milk by
the butter and cheese industries. It is expected that domestic demand
may result in purchase of butter abroad. Egg and poultry exports showed
a significant decline. British Ministry of Food egg purchases stopped
in December 1949 and exports to the United States dropped after the
first part of 1950. Domestic disappearance of both eggs and poultry
during 1950 was higher than for previous years, and consumer demand is
expected to continue to be high during 1951.

The fruit crop for 1950 was below that of 1949. Apples were 2½ million
bushels below the large 1949 crop. The soft fruit crops were very much
below normal, as a result of the winter damage in 1949-50. The upward
trend in production of soft tree-fruits was set back and low yields are
expected again during 1951.

The 1950 crops of soybeans and flaxseed were well above 1949, though the
production from minor oilseed crops, such as sunflowers and rape, were
very short due to farmers going out of their production. The potato crop
for 1950 was 97.4 million bushels, which is larger than the 1949 or the
1948 crops, and some difficulty is expected in its disposal.

UNITED STATES*

Summary: Despite less favorable growing conditions in 1950 than a year earlier, domestic food production was relatively large. As a result, total supplies of food in the United States were at a high level. The volume of agricultural production of food for sale and for farm home consumption was approximately equal to that of 1949 and 38 percent above the prewar (1935-39) annual average. Feed grain production in 1950 was high, so the production of livestock and livestock products probably will be maintained at a high level.

Civilian consumption of food per person in 1950 was the highest since 1947 and 12 percent above the prewar average annual rate. In terms of nutrients, slightly more calories per person were available to U.S. civilians in 1950 than in the prewar period; except for carbohydrates, which were smaller, important increases occurred in supplies of the other major nutrients, compared with the corresponding prewar average. Prospects for 1951 are that civilian per capita consumption of food both in terms of physical quantity and available nutrients, may average higher than in the preceding year, although lower than the record level reached in 1946. According to present indications, food exports during 1951 may not be much different than in the previous year.

1950 Production and 1951 Outlook: Meat production in 1950, totaling about 22.3 billion pounds (dressed meat basis), was greater than in either of the two preceding years but smaller than output during the years 1943 to 1947. Beef and pork production were somewhat higher than in 1949, but output of veal was smaller and that of lamb and mutton about the same. Most of the increase in meat output in 1950 occurred in pork because of larger pig crops both in 1949 and the spring of 1950.

Prospects for 1951 are that total meat supplies will be greater than in 1950, with most of the increase occurring in pork production. Some increase in civilian consumption per person is probable. Larger supplies of pork are likely to result from more hogs being slaughtered and possible slightly heavier weights. The latter would be a reversal of the slight shift downward toward higher average weights. Beef supplies in 1951 also may be a little larger than in 1950, but not much change in veal output is expected. Supplies of lamb and mutton, at a record low point in 1950, probably will continue small in 1951. Sheep growers are expected to hold back from the market increased numbers of live lambs for the purpose of building herds.

Supplies of fresh and frozen fishery products in 1950 were larger than a year earlier, with the increase principally in imports. Canned fish production was larger than in 1949. The very small production of canned salmon was more than offset by record output of canned tuna and both California and Maine sardines. Prospects for 1951 are that supplies of fishery products, except possibly for canned salmon, will be as favorable as in 1950. Canned salmon supplies will be smaller than in 1950 until at least the last quarter of the year when the 1951 pack will begin moving into distribution channels in large volume.

---

*Prepared by the Division of Statistical and Historical Research, Bureau of Agricultural Economics.

Farm and non-farm production of eggs in 1950 was a record at 5.4 billion dozen, 5 percent above output in the preceding year and about 2 percent greater than the previous record in 1944. This resulted from both an increase in the laying flock and a record egg output per bird. Production in 1951 may be somewhat smaller than in 1950, because of a smaller number of hens and pullets in laying flocks. Civilian consumption in 1950 is estimated at 390 eggs per person, higher than in any year since 1945. Exports of eggs, including substantial quantities of dried eggs from Government stocks, in 1950 were much larger than in the preceding two years. Production and total civilian consumption of poultry meat in 1950 was larger than a year earlier, and about 75 percent above the prewar (1935-39) annual average, with increases occurring both for chickens and turkeys. Prospective civilian consumption of eggs per person in 1951 will be about as large as a year earlier; exports probably will be no larger. Civilian consumption per capita of poultry in 1951 may be about equal to that in 1950.

The production of milk (including milk fed to calves) in 1950 was (123.3) billion pounds, slightly larger than a year earlier and second only to the 1945 record. The production of manufactured dairy products was approximately the same as in 1949, with declines noted for ice cream and butter and an increase for evaporated milk, dry skim and dry whole milk. Civilian consumption of fluid milk and cream in 1950 was 393 pounds per capita, slightly above the 1949 level. Total milk production in 1951 is not expected to differ much from that of a year earlier, but the pattern of milk utilization may be noticeably different, with more of the milk likely to be marketed for consumption as fluid milk, cream and ice cream, and declines likely for the quantity used in the production of butter.

Total production of fats and oils for food use (i.e., butter, lard, margarine, shortening and the fats and oils used in salad dressing, mayonnaise, salad oils and cooking oils) in 1950 was 8.5 billion pounds, slightly more than a year earlier and a record in volume. Increases from 1949 in the output of lard, margarine and shortening more than offset declines reported for butter and the other edible fats and oils. Imports of food fats and oils in 1950 remained relatively small, about 25 percent of the prewar (1935-39) average annual rate, while exports continued large, approximately four times the prewar annual level. Supplies of food fats and oils in 1951 will be sufficient to maintain the civilian consumption rate per person and exports at about the 1950 levels. Civilian consumption of these products in 1950 was 46 pounds (fat content) per person.

Supplies of fresh fruit in 1950 were the smallest since 1943, principally due to short crops caused by bad weather. Civilian consumption of fresh fruits in 1950 of about 110 pounds per person, was one of the lowest rates on record. But it was in part offset by increases in the per capita consumption of processed fruits. The pack of canned fruits was slightly larger than in 1949, and large stocks carried over from the 1949 pack maintained both total supplies and civilian consumption per capita at a high level. Supplies of frozen fruits and frozen fruit juices in 1950 were the largest on record; consumption by civilians reached the new

high of 4 pounds per person; Dried fruit output and supplies were
smallest since 1921, principally due to declines in the production
of prunes and raisins, but also due in part to the stronger demand
for $f_{r}u_i$ts in other forms.

More fresh vegetables were produced in 1950 than a year earlier
and civilian consumption, on a per person basis, increased slightly
from the 1949 rate of 249 pounds. Less canned vegetables were produced
in 1950 than a year earlier, but the large carry-over from the 1949 pack
supplemented production in 1950 and permitted civilians to consume about
a pound more canned vegetables than a year earlier. Frozen vegetable
production, which exceeded the 1949 output of 564 million pounds, was
a new record and supported the continued upward trend of civilian consumption per capita of these processed products.

The production of potatoes in 1950 totaled 439.5 million bushels,
about 7 percent above the previous crop and about 9 percent larger than
the annual output in 1939-48. As in the past few years, potato supplies
in 1950 exceeded domestic and export requirements, and substantial quantities were purchased by the U. S. Department of Agriculture under price-
support programs. Civilian consumption of potatoes in 1950 was the lowest on record. The 1950 crop of sweetpotatoes was 58.7 million bushels;
although 6 percent above the preceding crop, it was still somewhat smaller
than average. Sweetpotato consumption by civilians averaged 14.6 pounds
per capita, slightly above the 1949 rate but substantially smaller than
the prewar (1935-39) average annual level of 21.4 pounds. The dry edible
beans and pea crops in 1950 were smaller than those of a year earlier
and the corresponding average for 1939-48, but supplies are likely to
be sufficiently large to provide for domestic needs and for exports.

The 1950 wheat crop was 1,027 million bushels, about average in
size even though 10 percent smaller than in 1949. Total supplies for
the calendar year were sufficient to maintain civilian consumption at
the rate of 193 pounds per person (grain equivalent), to permit large
exports to be made, and to provide substantial stocks to be carried over
into 1951. Exports of wheat and wheat flour (grain equivalent basis) during the year were the smallest since 1945. The rice crop in the 1949-50
marketing year set a new record, but civilian consumption per person during this marketing year was the same as a year earlier, but below the prewar average. The rice crop to be marketed in 1950-51 totaled 38 million
hundred-pound units, 7 percent below the preceding year's record output
but more than one-fourth above average. A crop of this size will permit
civilian consumption rate per person to be maintained at about the same
rate as in 1949-50 (5.0 pounds, milled basis, per person) and still provide large supplies for export and carry-over stocks at the end of the
year.

Civilian disappearance of sugar during 1950 was 98.3 pounds (refined
basis) per person, the largest since 1941. Prospects for 1951 are that
supplies of sugar will be large enough to permit civilians to consume almost as much per person as in 1950. The marketing quota for 1951, recently
established at 8 million short tons (raw basis) by the Secretary of Agriculture, is designed to accomplish this purpose.

LATIN AMERICA

Increased supplies of foodstuffs for domestic consumption during 1950-51 are available in Latin American countries as a result of larger planted acreages. Considerably larger exportable surpluses of grain and meat in Argentina, rice in Brazil, and sugar in Cuba are moving abroad compared with the year before. Some increase in imports of foodstuffs are currently being permitted by those countries where favorable exchange balances have recently been accumulated.

By the middle of 1950 food supplies from domestic production were more plentiful in Latin America than in the preceding year, with the exception of the west coast of South America where adverse weather had seriously affected production. Available information indicates that per capita consumption of food reached an all-time high in practically every Latin American country, despite widespread inflation and unprecedentedly high prices. Improved weather conditions and larger acreages devoted to food crops indicate an even higher per capita consumption during 1950-51.

Argentina: Prospects for 1950-51 are for increased agricultural production. Crop and livestock conditions are generally better than the previous season, which may boost export supplies of principal foodstuffs and help minimize the seasonal declines in production of fresh milk and eggs. Thus far in the 1950-51 season meat exports have declined drastically owing to a price disagreement between Argentina and the United Kingdom. As a result, shipments for the year will probably be considerably below those of 1949-50, when over 500 thousand tons were exported. Wheat exports may show some increase, while corn and most other grains probably will be considerably above the exceptionally light movement of the previous season. Small exportable surpluses of vegetable oils and pulses are indicated for 1950-51. Rice production will about meet domestic requirements, but sugar output is expected to fall short of demand. Imports of coffee, bananas, and cacao, if the current rate of receipts is continued to the end of the season, will show little change from the previous year.

Domestic food supplies are somewhat more ample than a year ago and per capita consumption is probably even above the record high of 1949-50. Around 2 million tons of flour were consumed by Argentina's 17 million people during the past season. This high rate is expected to continue as long as the government's flour subsidy is in effect. Per capita consumption of meat was estimated at 243 pounds, an all-time high.

Brazil: Increased production of all major food commodities is indicated during 1950-51, with the exception of rice, which is expected to decline slightly due to reduced acreage. The wheat harvest, which began in December 1950, was materially larger than the previous one.

If imports to supplement domestic production continue at the same level as during the past season, per capita consumption will exceed the already record high level. The corn supply was relatively short until a record crop was harvested in early 1950. Farmers were discouraged

by declining rice prices following the 1950 harvest and consequently
planted a smaller acreage. As a result, the exportable surplus from the
1951 harvest may be relatively insignificant, and any exports during
1950-51 will probably be from carry-over of the previous crop. Sugar
production, which declined in 1949-50, is expected to recover to the
previous level, with significant quantities available for export.
Record crops of bananas, pineapples, papayas and some other fruits in
1949-50 may be surpassed by the current production.

Beef production in 1949-50 was curtailed by drought. Rains in
mid-1950 have now improved pastures and a larger beef supply is in
prospect for 1951. The production of pork and mutton increased slightly
over the year before. Ample supplies of corn during the last half of
1950 resulted in heavier hogs and a larger number for slaughter in 1951.
With a production of 100 thousand tons and relatively insignificant
exports, consumption of vegetable oils is currently at record level. It
will probably decline by the second quarter of 1951, however, due to a
short cotton crop.

Uruguay: Indications thus far in the 1950-51 season are that total
agricultural output is about the same as the previous year. Exports,
consisting principally of meat and edible oilseeds, during the current
season are expected to equal those of 1949-50 which were the highest
in more than 10 years. Other commodities received in substantial
quantities were yerba mate, bananas, and coffee. The high level of
imports is expected to continue through 1950-51.

Supplies of most foodstuffs have been fairly abundant in Uruguay
despite a summer drought and a packing house strike which temporarily
paralyzed the meat industry. Sheep and cattle slaughterings were at
high levels except for three months in mid-1950. Production of food
grains more than met domestic demands and supplies were available for
export. Consumption of beef, mutton, rice, wheat, and sugar was at
record levels, but domestic disappearance of pork, pulses, and edible
oils was below average.

Chile: High prices and prospects of good yields have encouraged
farmers to plant larger acreages of many food crops for harvest in
1950-51. Accordingly, prospects are excellent for an overall food
output considerably above the previous season, which was roughly 10
percent below 1948-49. Production of fruit crops will probably be close
to normal although some frost damage has been reported. Poor pasture,
as a result of last summer's drought, is now seriously reducing the meat
supply. Less meat is available during the 1950-51 season at a relatively
higher price than in 1949-50, but recent rains may raise milk production
slightly above the previous year.

Exports, which dropped off by 30 percent, are expected to show
some recovery after the current crops are harvested. Significant exports
will probably be confined to pulses and fruits. Only the most essential
imports have been permitted to enter Chile for more than a year.
Authorized food imports are restricted principally to cattle, sheep,
bananas, coffee, cacao, vegetable oils, and sugar. Heavy wheat imports
probably will be required before the next crop is harvested.

Peru: Food supplies are adequate in most areas and temporary shortages
have been caused by inadequate distribution rather than lack of supplies.
Imports of wheat and flour, meat, rice, and vegetable oils are being
permitted to augment local production. Although sugar production has
been reduced by adverse weather, supplies are proving sufficient for
domestic requirements. Export restrictions prevent food stocks, except
sugar and coffee, from leaving the country. Nearly adequate food
supplies will be available for the remainder of the 1950-51 season, but
at continually increasing prices. Controls on both imports and exports
can be expected to continue indefinitely.

Colombia: The current consumption year, beginning August 1, 1950,
commenced at the height of a food shortage situation following a period
of poor harvests. Emergency food supplies imported under a Government
program began to arrive shortly after this date. By the end of 1950
the supply situation had improved to the extent that imports had been
cut back sharply and prices had stabilized. Prospects are that imports
will be further reduced as domestic production gradually improves with a
return to normal weather conditions. Sugar production is rising and there
is the likelihood that Colombia will be prepared to enter the world
market on a somewhat larger scale following the 1951 harvest. Rice
acreage has increased to the point at which fair quantities should
be exportable provided the output of other food crops is satisfactory.
Large quantities of bananas are currently being exported.   —

Central American Countries: With the exception of El Salvador, all the
countries of Central America are in somewhat better position now with
respect to food supplies for domestic consumption than they were a year
ago. By and large, this area is self-sufficient in the production of
corn, beans, and rice, the three staple articles of the local diet.
Deficits in one country are usually offset by surpluses in another. The
area as a whole imports wheat and wheat flour, fats and oils, and
processed milk, and exports bananas and cacao. Little change is expected
in this normal situation during the 1950-51 season.

Mexico: In spite of the drought in the central and northern districts
of Mexico this past year, total food production exceeded the output in
1949. As a result of larger area planted and better yield per acre, corn
production in 1950 is estimated at 106 million bushels, compared with
91 million last year. It was, however, smaller than the record crop
of 1948. Because of the short crop last year, carry-overs are negligible
and total supply of corn for the current consumption year will be tight.
The production of wheat, rice, barley, bananas, pineapples, sugar, and
fats and oils were also higher in 1950. A lower production is indicated
for beans, chickpeas, tomatoes, and oats. In 1950-51, Mexico is continuing
to import wheat, fats and oils, and powdered milk. Principal exportable
surpluses are rice, chickpeas, bananas, tomatoes, pineapples, and sugar.
(Table in Appendix)

During the past few months there have been heavier-than-normal
imports of wheat to maintain food consumption at previous levels. This
together with supplies of corn from the winter crop, may obviate the
necessity of importing any corn during 1950-51. Rice and sugar production

continue to expand and exports of 120 million pounds and 55 thousand short tons respectively are forecast for the 1950-51 period.

Cattlemen in northern Mexico have almost completed reorganization of their ranges to conform to the changed conditions which resulted from the closing of the border at the end of 1946. Beef production for export in 1950-51 will be somewhat above that for the preceeding year. Virtually no beef has been canned in Mexico since January 1950. On the domestic market the outlook is for continued normal supplies of fresh beef and pork in the major consuming centers.

Caribbean Area: Food supplies in the Caribbean, particularly in Cuba, the Dominican Republic, and Haiti were plentiful during 1949-50 and domestic consumption was probably at a record level. With some increase in crop acreages an even higher level of food consumption is expected during 1950-51. As a result of an increase in sugarcane acreage in Cuba, some increase in production is expected in 1950-51 in comparison with the previous year, but the effect of adverse weather conditions will probably keep the harvest below the record outturn of 1947-48. Substantial increases in sugar output are also anticipated from other Caribbean countries.

Exports during 1949-50 consisted largely of sugar and tropical fruits, while rice, wheat flour, processed milk, and fats and oils made up most of the imports into this area. Both exports and imports are expected to show substantial increases in 1950-51.

THE SITUATION BY COMMODITIES 1/

CEREALS

The world grain situation at the beginning of 1951 is characterized by three consecutive years (1948, 1949 and 1950) of relatively favorable production, a reasonable over-all balance between supplies and requirements, but some concern over the utilization and distribution of available supplies in the light of current international developments. World trade in bread grains (wheat and rye) during the 1950-51 marketing season is expected to be slightly less than in 1949-50, but more of the wheat trade will come under the International Wheat Agreement. For rice, world supplies and requirements are expected to show very little change in total from the level of a year ago, unless developments in the important Far Eastern rice countries affect trade movement. Supplies of feed grains available for international trade this season are centered largely in North America, particularly the United States. Some decline from last year's level of world trade is indicated despite increased feed needs.

Bread grains: The 1950 world harvest of bread grains (wheat and rye) is estimated at about 239 million short tons, only slightly below the record world crop in 1948. The current estimate is a little larger than the 1949 outturn as well as above the immediate prewar average of 229 million tons, with increases in the wheat crop only partly offset by declines for rye. Production was up one-third above prewar in North America and about 10 percent in Asia. Moderate deficits compared with prewar, estimated for Europe and the Soviet Union, however, partially offset those increases.

The production pattern, by continents, is shown in the following table:

Breadgrain production, 1950 with comparisons 1/

Year	North America	Europe	U.S.S.R.	Asia	Africa	South America	Oceania	World total
	Thousand short tons							
Av. 1935-39	34,090	69,420	61,980	45,360	4,320	8,740	5,310	229,220
1946	48,170	53,570	43,400	48,060	4,335	8,560	3,695	209,790
1947	52,840	43,900	52,100	46,230	3,870	10,220	6,750	215,910
1948	53,055	62,130	56,790	48,475	4,530	8,470	5,910	239,360
1949	46,740	65,030	59,600	44,640	4,740	8,680	6,690	236,120
1950	46,280	65,080	58,780	49,515	4,525	9,310	5,850	239,340

1/ Estimated production of wheat and rye.

1/ Tables showing production by countries of the commodities referred to in this section of the World Food Situation were included in world summary articles published at scheduled intervals during 1950 by the Office of Foreign Agricultural Relations in the weekly publication Foreign Crops and Markets, or as Foreign Agriculture Circulars.

The European crop of wheat and rye, estimated at 65.1 million short tons, was virtually unchanged from the 1949 total, which represented the largest production of the postwar period. The current crop was, however, still about 6 percent below the 1935-39 average. That reduction was attributed to the low level of acreage which, though showing some recovery from the small 1949 area, remained somewhat below the prewar level. Yields per acre for Europe, as a whole, were a little above average though not generally up to the high yields in 1949. Yields in western Europe, the Iberian Peninsula, and the United Kingdom were mostly well above average, offsetting lower yields in most of eastern and central Europe.

Relatively unfavorable harvests were reported in the Danube Basin countries, where drought appears to have reduced yields somewhat below average, though the full effects of the drought were felt after the harvest of small grains was completed. Yields in central Europe were mostly below average, but in Germany yields were above average on a smaller acreage, bringing the total cutturn near the prewar average. It is noted that cutturns appeared best in normally deficit areas of the Continent and least favorable in the Danube countries, traditionally an exporting area.

The breadgrain crop in the Soviet Union is estimated about 5 percent below the prewar average and also slightly smaller than the 1949 harvest. The reduction from the prewar figure appears to have occurred in the wheat crop, with rye production indicated to be above the average. This is believed to be largely the result of some net shift from wheat to rye acreage which occurred during the later war years, and which has been maintained in the postwar period. A substantial increase was reported in spring wheat acreage in 1950 and served to maintain wheat production near the 1949 total despite below-average yields.

The breadgrain harvest in Asia is estimated at about 50 million short tons. This would be about 10 percent larger than last year's slightly below-average crop. Rye is of little significance in this area, with Turkey the only country of any importance in rye production. The wheat cutturn is estimated at 48.9 million short tons, compared with the 1935-39 average of 44.9 million tons. A large part of the increase is attributed to increased acreage, especially in China and Turkey. Yields were around average in most important producing areas and, especially in Turkey, were much above the low yields of a year ago.

Production in other continents, Africa, South America, and Oceania, normally amounts to less than 10 percent of the world total. Production in these areas in 1950 was above average though not up to the high 1949 level.

1951 Outlook: Prospects for bread grains sown in the fall of 1950 for harvest in 1951 in Europe were variable at latest report, with unfavorable weather during seeding time in a number of countries. Excessive rains held up seeding in many areas, especially during November, and may result in some reduction in winter grain acreage. Actual estimates of areas seeded are available for very few countries, but general indications of conditions in the principal producing countries denote little change in acreage expected.

The acreage seeded to winter wheat in France up to January 1 was 9.5 million acres, about 4 percent less than on that date of 1949. Rye acreage was also slightly smaller than that of a year ago. Though spring plantings are expected to make up most of the shortfall in winter grain acreage, the total breadgrain acreage there is not expected to show any significant change from that of the 1950 crop. The condition of the winter grain was good at the beginning of December on the basis of official reports. Trade reports since that time have noted the continuation of favorable conditions. The outlook is favorable in Italy, with little change from last year's acreage expected. Seeding has been backward in parts of Spain because of dryness in some areas. A 5 percent increase had been expected in that country's grain acreage. Planting intentions in Western Germany called for a small net increase in winter greadgrain acreage, with increased wheat acreage more than compensating for reduced acreage of winter rye. Seeding of winter grain has been delayed by heavy rains in the United Kingdom, and trade sources suggest that extensive spring planting would be necessary if the goal of 2.55 million acres is to be reached. Little information is available on the seeding progress in central Europe and the Balkan countries. The drought in the latter area was reported broken in early October, facilitating preparation of the land for fall seeding. Heavy rains in the low countries and in Scandinavia are reported to have made some reduction in fall grain acreage in those countries.

The Soviet Union reported sowing of fall grain accomplished early, with some increase over the 1949 sowings.

In the United States the acreage of winter wheat seeded for all purposes is estimated at 56.1 million acres. This estimate of winter wheat acreage indicates an increase of 6 percent over the acreage seeded in the fall of 1949 for harvest in 1950 and is 17 percent above the average for the 10 years ended 1948. Increased acreage was reported for all areas except the South Atlantic and East South Central groups of States. In general, late summer and early fall weather conditions were favorable, giving the 1951 crop a good start. Despite deterioration of crop conditions over much of the Great Plains area since late September because of near-depletion of surface soil moisture, prospects were still favorable as of December 1. A possible outturn of about 900 million bushels of winter wheat was then in prospect for 1951, assuming normal weather for the remainder of the crop season. This, if achieved, would be the third largest crop of record and would be 20 percent larger than the winter wheat harvest in 1950. Winter wheat acreage in the United States has represented about 70 percent of total wheat acreage in recent years. Canada's winter wheat acreage, in contrast, is normally only about 5 percent of the total. The current acreage in Canada is placed at 918,000 acres, a decline of 12 percent from last year's sowings. Fall rye acreage of 867,000 acres is down about 6 percent from the previous acreage.

Little official information is available regarding the crop outlook in Asia. At latest report, the wheat acreage in India was in need of moisture in some areas, especially in the Northwest, according to trade sources. Conditions elsewhere in the country were reported satisfactory. No information is available on winter grain prospects in China, the principal winter wheat producer of Asia.

World Trade (Wheat and Rye): Present indications are that world trade in wheat and rye during the 1950-51 marketing season will total about 5 percent less than the 1949-50 level of approximately 26.3 million short tons. Practically all of this trade will be in wheat and wheat flour since rye has accounted for a relatively small part (5 percent or less) of total world trade in bread grains thus far in the postwar period. Of the total, about 16.2 million short tons - or 65 percent - are expected to be traded under the International Wheat Agreement, with some indication that this percentage may be increased before the year is out. Stabilized prices and assured sources of supply under the Agreement are assuming increasing importance as factors of trade in importing countries. All important deficit areas, except Japan, are now covered by the International Wheat Agreement.

The major postwar adjustment of world trade in bread grains occurred in the 1949-50 season, when exports declined substantially from the near-record level of the 1948-49 season. This adjustment was reflected largely in reduced exports of wheat and flour from the United States, but further declines from the 300 million bushel total of wheat and flour exports from this country are expected to be limited during the current shipping season. Because of some reduction in the expected availability of wheat from non-dollar sources, transportation difficulties in Canada, and extraordinary requirements in areas such as Yugoslavia and India, it now appears that 1950-51 exports of wheat and flour from the United States will exceed earlier expectations of 250 million bushels by as much as 10 percent or more. The extent of the increase will depend to a large extent on the availability of dollar exchange to finance imports from this country.

Export availabilities of bread grains from the other principal exporting countries during 1950-51 are expected to show little change from a year ago. This does not include an allowance for significant quantities of low-quality wheat which will be available for export from Canada later in the marketing season. In Australia, reduced supplies of wheat for export from the 1950-51 crop will be augmented by an increased carry-over from production of the previous year. Any increase in availability in Argentina will be limited to the crop recently harvested, since carry-over on December 1, 1950, was reported to be at minimum levels. Some reduction from the 1949-50 total of rye exports from eastern Europe is expected during the current year. Exports of wheat from the Soviet Union and Danube Basin are also moving at a reduced rate thus far in the 1950-51 marketing season.

The principal reasons for the expected decline in world trade in bread grains during the 1950-51 year are reduced takings in most of the traditionally deficit countries of western Europe as a result of increased domestic supplies and further declines in consumption. Much better harvests, particularly in Turkey, will also remove that country, and probably Iran, from the list of importing countries in the current season as compared with 1949-50, when over 600,000 tons were exported to those two countries. On balance, the declines will more than offset expected increases in import requirements in other countries, including extraordinary demands from such countries as Yugoslavia and India resulting from unfavorable domestic production.

Rice

  Production: One of the world's largest rice crops is being harvested in the 1950-51 (August-July) crop year. Production in terms of milled rice is estimated at 119,000,000 short tons compared with 116,700,000 tons in 1949-50 and the prewar average (1935-36/39-40) of 117,200,000 short tons. Despite the increase in production from prewar, however, the per capita consumption of rice is less because of the gain in population in the heavy rice-consuming countries of the world.

  The total production of Asia, representing 92 percent of the world crop, is larger than in the preceding year, and 2 percent less than before World War II. The harvest is below expectations this year because of drought conditions in northeastern India, which caused a substantial reduction in that country's crop.

  The high postwar level of production generally is being maintained in the continents other than Asia. Their combined harvest is about 4,500,000 tons, or 85 percent larger than before World War II. Europe's record production in 1950 increased 15 percent from the prewar average and exceeded by 11 percent the previous record of a year earlier. Although decreases are forecast in both North and South America, compared with the year before, their total production is 78 and 86 percent, respectively, larger than the prewar average. Indications are that Africa's production is about the same as in the preceding year, and 63 percent larger than before the war.

  Trade: World exportable supplies during 1951 from the 1950-51 crop are forecast at about the same level as, or perhaps slightly exceeding, the exports of a year earlier. These supplies are estimated in terms of milled rice at about the same level as the preliminary estimate of actual exports in 1950 of 4,600,000 short tons. The total volume exported in 1950 was considerably above expectations because of the procurement of several hundred thousand tons of stocks from the interior of Burma, when transportation difficulties were largely overcome.

  Exporting Countries: Asia's exporting countries in 1951 are expected to supply approximately 70 percent of the world's exportable surplus of rice, with 63 percent centered in the so-called "rice bowl" of Asia, Burma, Thailand, and Indochina (Cambodia, Laos, and Vietnam). Exportable supplies in this region are estimated at 2,950,000 short tons of milled rice, compared with 2,840,000 short tons in the preceding year and 6,300,000 tons before the war (1936-40).

  Thailand is the only one of these countries where acreage and production have been restored to the prewar average. Burma's acreage is only 72 percent, and its exports only 40 percent, of the prewar level. Good crops are being harvested in these countries, and the exportable supplies are forecast at about the same level as 1950 exports.

RICE (in terms of milled): Production and exports in principal exporting countries, average 1935/36 to 1939/40, annual 1949/50 and 1950/51 1/

Continent and country	Production			Exports	
	1935/36 to 1939/40	1949/50	1950/51	1936 to 1940	2/ 1950
	- - - 1,000 short tons - - -				
Western Hemisphere					
North America:					
United States........ :	729	1,304	1,195	107	540
Mexico................ :	59	132	163	9	45
Others................ :	123	257	263	-	15
Estimated total					
North America.... :	911	1,693	1,621	116	600
South America:					
Brazil............... :	971	2,067 3/	-	42	100
British Guiana....... :	52	72 3/	-	17	25
Ecuador.............. :	50	121 3/	-	13	55
Others............... :	228	383 3/	-	8	20
Estimated total					
South America.... :	1,301	2,643	2,415	80	200
Estimated total					
Western Hemisphere:	2,212	4,336	4,036	196	800
Asia					
Indochina..............	5,039	4,253	3,896	1,610	90
Thailand...............	3,356	4,148	4,165	1,460	1,450
Burma..................	5,489	3,145	3,150	3,268	1,300
Korea..................	3,083	4/2,392 3/	-	1,061	4/ 100
Taiwan.................	1,350	1,295	1,400	709	250
Others................ :	93,663	92,697 3/	-	32	60
Estimated total Asia. :	111,980	107,930	110,000	8,140	3,205
Europe					
Italy.................. :	550	484	537	168	200
Estimated total Europe:	778	812	904	170	210
Africa					
Egypt................. :	524	901	910	132	330
Estimated total Africa:	1,743	2,848	2,848	156	340
Estimated World total :	117,240	116,700	119,000	8,700	4,600

1/ For countries of Asia and Africa, rough rice is converted to terms of milled at 70 percent, for other countries at 65 percent. 2/ Preliminary estimate. 3/ Unavailable. 4/ South Korea only.

Compiled in the Office of Foreign Agricultural Relations, January 8, 1951.

Although the surplus available for export from Indochina is estimated at 200,000 short tons, larger stocks may exist in the Transbassac area of South Vietnam. The exportation of any sizable quantity, even up to this volume, depends on several factors: (1) the repeal of the current decree which prohibits exports; (2) the lifting of the Transbassac blockade; and (3) political and military factors.

Formosa should have some surplus from its record crop of 1950-51. Despite a natural increase in population and also immigration from China, production is estimated to be sufficient for domestic requirements and to permit the exportation of rice to other countries.

The exportable supplies in countries other than in Asia represent about 30 percent of the world total exports. Proportionately, these availabilities exist in the following continents: North America (principally the United States), 13 percent; South America (Brazil and Ecuador), 4 percent; Europe (Italy), 5 percent; and Africa (Egypt), 7 percent.

Rice exports from the surplus countries of the Western Hemisphere in 1951 also probably will approximate those of 1950, both in North and South America. Although a smaller acreage was planted in the United States, the yields per acre were considerably higher and the harvest, therefore, was nearly as large as in the year before. Export supplies in Mexico show a moderate increase over those of a year ago.

Rice production statistics for most South American countries are not yet available, since the harvest will not be completed for some months. Present indications are that total production will be less than in 1950, but the expected reduction in current crop supplies in 1951 may be partly offset by carry-over of stocks from the 1950 crop.

Production in Brazil, South America's largest producer and exporter of rice, is reported to be less than last year. Prospects indicate that, because of the reduction in the harvest, the surplus, if any, from the 1951 crop may be reduced from the export availabilities of the 1950 harvest. Some of the unshipped surplus of last season's crop, however, probably will be exported during the 1951 calendar year.

Climatic conditions in Italy and Egypt, the principal areas of export in Europe and Africa, were beneficial for rice production, and since large acreages were planted again, the production was at a high level, and the export surpluses approximate the relatively large availabilities in 1950, estimated at 340,000 and 200,000 tons, respectively.

Importing Countries: In recent years about 80 percent of the world's rice surplus has been imported into the deficit countries of Asia. These principally were Japan, India, and China. Sizable imports are required also in Ceylon, Malaya, Indonesia, and lesser quantities in Hong Kong and the Philippines.

Japan's requirements will continue to be heavy, since even the volume imported before the war has been unavailable in postwar years. India's needs will be substantially larger in 1951 than in 1950, because of a severe reduction in some areas on account of floods. The other importing countries of the world will require at least the volume imported in 1949 (see table in statistical appendix).

RICE (in terms of milled);. Production and imports in principal importing
countries, average 1935/36 to 1939/40; annual 1949/50 and 1950/51

Continent and country	Production			Imports		
	1935/36 to 1939/40	1949/50	1950/51	1936 to 1940	1948	1949
		- - - 1,000 short tons - - -				
Western Hemisphere						
North America:						
Canada............	0	0	0	25	20	25
Cuba.............	14	44	44	222	259	299
Estimated total North America....	-	-	-	345	329	373
Estimated total South America....	-	-	-	103	36	27
Asia						
Ceylon...........	205	218	256	610	458	445
China............	38,630	34,335	38,500	435	425	1/450
India............	26,160	26,507	2/ -	1,863	980	860
Japan............	9,378	9,743	8,995	2,061	62	3/150
Malaya...........	427	498	455	873	509	567
Indonesia........	10,250	10,000	2/ -	250	202	271
Philippines......	1,652	1,999	2,055	65	132	160
Estimated total Asia:	111,980	107,930	110,000	6,996	3,526	4/ -
Europe						
United Kingdom...	0	0	0	156	47	59
Germany..........	0	0	0	242	31	52
France...........	5/ -	16	22	620	38	47
Belgium..........	0	0	0	70	11	30
Estimated total Europe...........	-		-	1,632	182	297

1/ Estimated.
2/ Unavailable.
3/ Imports into Japan during 1949 were not permitted by I.E.F.C.
Imports in 1950, however, are estimated at 660,000 tons.
4/ Not greatly different from imports of 1948.
5/ Less than 500 tons.

Compiled in the Office of Foreign Agricultural Relations,
January 15, 1951.

Coarse Grains

Production: The world production of coarse grains (corn, oats, and barley) in 1950 is estimated at 274 million short tons. This is about the same as the 1949 total for these crops. The current estimate is about 6 percent above the 1935-39 average, but is somewhat below the record harvest in 1948. The increase over the prewar average occurred principally in North America, which has accounted for about half the world total for these grains in recent years. Substantial increases in the United States corn and oats crops account for the bulk of the expansion over the prewar average. Estimated totals for these crops are below the prewar level in Europe and in the Soviet Union. The coarse grain production in Europe is also less than the 1949 harvest. Changes in areas other than those mentioned are of minor importance.

Coarsegrain production, 1950 with comparisons 1/

Year	Area or continent							
	North America	Europe	U.S.S.R.	Asia	Africa	South America	Oceania	World total
	Thousand short tons							
Av. 1935-39	98,270	61,225	33,600	36,930	10,395	18,005	970	259,395
1946	135,310	46,165	15,970	35,045	9,920	16,800	875	260,085
1947	105,210	51,180	25,120	36,505	10,615	17,005	1,635	247,270
1948	149,215	55,770	23,820	37,545	10,590	15,310	1,190	293,440
1949	134,030	56,720	23,760	35,775	11,445	11,340	1,310	274,380
1950	134,530	52,440	24,000	37,075	10,525	14,135	1,265	273,970

1/ Estimated production of barley, oats, and corn.

Trade: Supplies of coarse grains(corn, oats, barley, and grain sorghums) available for export during the 1950-51 year are centered largely in North America, particularly in the United States. This is a result of unfavorable harvests in other surplus-producing regions such as Argentina, where the corn crop harvested in March-June 1950, failed even to meet normal domestic requirements. In prewar years, Argentina was the world's principal source of supply for feedgrains, but a sharply lower level of corn acreage since World War II has reduced exports from that country to less than half the prewar average of over 7.5 million short tons.

Total exports of coarse grains from Argentina in 1949-50 (July-June) were approximately 1.9 million short tons, and, with near-failure of the corn crop, feedgrain exports from that country during the current season are not likely to exceed 1.0 million tons. Exports from the Soviet Union are at a reduced rate, compared with a year ago, and drought in the Danube Basin may place that area on a net import basis for the year. Supplies of coarse grains (principally barley) for export from French North Africa are expected to be less than a year ago, while supplies in the Middle East are reported to be somewhat larger, especially in Turkey.

World exports of coarse grains totalled about 12.5 million short tons in 1949-50, of which about 4.5 million came from the United States. Even though a substantial increase in shipments is expected from this country during the 1950-51 season, present indications are that world trade in this group of commodities will not reach the total of the previous year. Western Europe will be the principal destination for supplies of coarse grains from the United States, but significant quantities will also move to India (grain sorghums for feed) and to Japan.

SUGAR.

World production of centrifugal 1/cane and beet sugar in 1950-51 is expected to total 35.5 million short tons, raw value, or about 10 percent more than in 1949-50 and 20 percent above the 5-year (1935-39) average.

The production of non-centrifugal 1/ sugar is expected to total 5.7 million short tons, tel quel (as produced), in 1950-51 compared with 6.2 million tons in 1949-50 and the 5-year (1935-39) average of 4.9 million tons.

Centrifugal sugar production in North and Central America and the West Indies in 1950-51 is expected to total 12.8 million short tons compared with 11.9 million tons in 1949-50 and the prewar average of 7.8 million tons. Production in this area has been relatively high since 1946-47 and this season's output may set a new high record. Production of non-centrifugal sugar in this area is indicated at 313,000 tons compared with 307,000 tons in 1949-50 and the prewar average of 163,000 tons. The large output in prospect gives promise of ample supplies for the Western Hemisphere and an increased availability for export to the remainder of the world.

For Europe, excluding the Soviet Union, sugar production in 1950-51 is expected to total 8.9 million tons, an increase of 1.4 million over last year's output. It may exceed the wartime average by 2.3 million tons and the 5-year (1935-39) prewar average by 1.6 million tons. Although consumption in the area may increase somewhat, the increased production prospect indicates that the new import requirements may be reduced somewhat from that of the 1949-50 season. Other factors affecting the continuance of imports are the increasing availability of dollar exchange for the purchase of sugar in the Western Hemisphere and the desire by importing countries to enhance stocks.

Sugar production in the Soviet Union has been increasing slowly during the last few years and is expected to continue the trend in 1950-51. Production is expected to total 2.3 million tons compared with the 5-year (1935-39) average for the comparable area of 2.8 million tons. In recent years the Soviet Union has imported sizeable quantities from Eastern Germany, Czechoslovakia, Hungary and Poland under compensation agreements and reparation arrangements.

In Asia the output of centrifugal sugar is forecast at 4.2 million short tons compared with 3.5 million in 1949-50 and the prewar average of 5.9 million tons. The prospect for Indonesia and Formosa is still far below the prewar output. For the area as a whole prospects indicate a total production of non-centrifugal sugar of 4.1 million tons compared with 4.7 million tons in 1949-50 and the prewar average of 4.0 million

---

1/ See notes on accompanying tables for definitions.

tons. In India and Pakistan where the bulk of this type of sugar is produced, the estimates are for net production of gur. The export availability is expected to be increased sharply in the Philippines and only
slightly in Indonesia but decreased in Formosa.

In South America sugar prospects are good and the upward trend of
production which has been evident during the last few years is continuing.
Total production of centrifugal sugar in 1950-51 is placed at 3.3 million
tons compared with 3.1 million in 1949-50 and the prewar average of 2.0
million. For the non-centrifugal type, production is estimated at 1.3
million tons in 1950-51 or about the same as a year earlier and compares
with 709,000 tons, the prewar average. With the exception of British
Guiana and a part of the output in Peru, most of the sugar produced in
this area is consumed domestically or in neighboring areas.

Sugar production in Africa is expected to total 1.7 million tons in
1950-51 or slightly more than in 1949-50 and compares with the prewar
average of 1.3 million tons. The Continent, as a whole, is approximately
in balance on supplies and requirements, but much of the production of
Mauritius and the Portuguese Colonies is shipped out while the French
Colonies and Egypt import from abroad.

In Oceania sugar production has been increasing during the postwar
years and this trend is expected to continue in 1950-51. Production is
now forecast at 2.4 million tons compared with 2.2 million tons in
1949-50 and the prewar average of 2.1 million tons. About one-half of
the Australia-Fiji Islands production is usually exported to the United
Kingdom, or some of the other British Dominions, while most of the
Hawaiian output is shipped to the United States.

PART I. CENTRIFUGAL SUGAR (raw value): Production in specified countries, averages 1935-39, 1940-44, and annual 1947-50 1/ 2/

Continent and country	Average 1935-39	Average 1940-44	1947	1948	1949	1950 3/
	- - - - - - - - 1,000 short tons - - - - - - - - - - -					
NORTH AMERICA						
Mexico	354:	450:	714:	754:	712:	800
United States	1,992:	1,880:	2,208:	1,847:	2,084:	2,564
Cuba	3,183:	3,686:	6,675:	5,763:	6,126:	6,300
Dominican Republic ..	491:	494:	465:	527:	524:	560
Puerto Rico	974:	961:	1,108:	1,277:	1,286:	1,275
British West Indies .	468:	453:	472:	672:	728:	778
French West Indies ..	125:	87:	56:	80:	113:	140
Others	189:	233:	262:	289:	325:	378
Total North America	7,776:	8,244:	11,960:	11,209:	11,898:	12,795
EUROPE						
Czechoslovakia	715:	680:	387:	699:	690:	800
France	1,059:	643:	732:	1,058:	972:	1,350
Germany	1,620:	1,600:	863:	1,431:	1,301:	1,750
Italy	426:	422:	270:	502:	556:	600
Poland	1,000:	870:	606:	765:	909:	1,000
United Kingdom	527:	560:	534:	696:	575:	725
Others	1,990:	1,839:	1,605:	2,331:	2,529:	2,652
Total (excl. USSR) .	7,337:	6,614:	4,997:	7,482:	7,532:	8,877
USSR (Europe & Asia).	2,761:	1,350:	1,700:	2,000:	2,200:	2,300
ASIA						
India	1,300:	1,410:	1,416:	1,319:	1,251:	1,560
Formosa	1,202:	921:	290:	697:	675:	450
Indonesia	1,447:	953:	100:	249:	300:	500
Philippine Islands ..	1,058:	320:	398:	729:	680:	1,000
Others	870:	833:	682:	734:	631:	651
Total Asia	5,877:	4,437:	2,886:	3,728:	3,537:	4,161
SOUTH AMERICA						
Argentina	480:	480:	668:	623:	605:	675
Brazil	786:	958:	1,496:	1,549:	1,500:	1,550
British Guiana	209:	189:	194:	196:	222:	225
Peru	430:	463:	520:	518:	475:	500
Others	121:	170:	223:	279:	329:	339
Total South America	2,026:	2,260:	3,101:	3,165:	3,131:	3,289
AFRICA						
Egypt	167:	190:	245:	210:	193:	200
Mauritius	321:	330:	384:	432:	459:	490
Union of South Africa	478:	550:	512:	608:	561:	600
Others	308:	303:	357:	367:	398:	416
Total Africa	1,274:	1,373:	1,498:	1,617:	1,611:	1,706
OCEANIA						
Australia and Fiji ..	1,037:	876:	834:	1,205:	1,193:	1,272
Hawaiian Islands	980:	880:	835:	956:	960:	1,085
Japanese Mandated Is.	69:	30:	0:	0:	0:	0
Total Oceania	2,086:	1,786:	1,669:	2,161:	2,153:	2,357
WORLD TOTAL	29,137:	26,064:	27,811:	31,362:	32,062:	35,485

PART II. NON CENTRIFUGAL-SUGAR: Production in specified countries, averages 1935-39, 1940-44, annual 1947-50 4/ 2/ .

Continent and country	Average		1947	1948	1949	1950 3/
	1935-39	1940-44				
	1,000 short tons	1,000 short tons	1,000 short tons	1,000 short tons	1,000 short tons	1,000 short tons
CENTRAL AMERICA						
Mexico.............:	83	141	181	171	180	180
Others ....:	80	113	125	139	127	133
Total Central America:	163	254	306	310	307	313
ASIA						
India.............:	3,215	3,060	3,379	3,371	3,691	3,125
Pakistan..........:	660	610	740	835	840	850
Others ....:	166	226	134	132	131	131
Total Asia.........:	4,041	3,896	4,253	4,338	4,662	4,106
SOUTH AMERICA						
Brazil............:	205	431	417	417	420	420
Colombia..........:	420	540	758	700	650	650
Others............:	84	137	134	182	202	205
Total South America..:	709	1,108	1,309	1,299	1,272	1,275
World total...........:	4,913	5,258	5,868	5,947	6,241	5,694

1/ Centrifugal sugar, as distinguished from non-centrifugal, includes cane and beet sugar produced by the centrifugal process, which is the principal kind moving in international trade. 2/ Years shown are for crop years; generally the harvesting season begins in the fall months of the year shown or in the early months of the following year, except in certain cane-sugar producing countries in the Southern Hemisphere, such as Australia, Argentina, Mauritius, Union of South Africa, etc., where the season begins in May or June of the year shown. 3/ Preliminary. 4/ Non-centrifugal sugar includes all types of sugar produced by other than the centrifugal process which is largely for consumption in the relatively few areas where produced. The estimates include such kinds as piloncillo, panelo, chancaca, rapadura, jaggery, gur, muscovado, panocha, pepelon, etc.

EDIBLE PULSES

The 1950-51 aggregate production of dry edible beans, peas, lentils and chickpeas, (garbanzos both food and feed types) in the major producing countries is estimated at 308 million bags of 100 pounds. This is 7 percent below the estimated production of last year and 5 percent more than the annual average in the prewar years 1935-39.

All of the decline from last year occurred in chickpeas, beans, and peas. The 1950 production of lentils increased from last year by 700,000 bags or 13 percent. The major decline,which was in chickpeas, was 13 percent below 1949 and only 3 percent above prewar. Beans and peas were down only 5 and 3 percent respectively. India was the principal country affected by the chickpea decline as chickpeas are in plentiful supply in Mexico and reasonably plentiful in most other producing areas.

Several months ago there was a surplus of about 750,000 bags of old-crop chickpeas. This surplus, while significant to the Mexican market, from the standpoint of world supply was insignificant in comparison with the decline of production in India where the 1950 crop was estimated at 15 million bags below 1949.

A sizeable carry-over of beans was reported near the end of the consumption year in the United States. No other carry-overs were reported elsewhere in the world. There were probably few, if any, as supplies in non-dollar areas likely moved into consumption before the end of the 1949-50 consumption year. United States bean stocks as of last September 1, were estimated at about 10 million bags. These, together with the Mexican chickpea stocks, as estimated a few months ago, would total only about 3 percent of the 1950 aggregate pulse production.

Considering this relatively small carry-over together with the small 5 percent increase of aggregate world pulse production since prewar, and comparing it with the population increase of about 14 percent or more, the 1950-51 per capita supply of pulses in the world appears to be somewhat below normal. But considering the shifts in the production of the various kinds of pulses, the taste preferences that exist for certain kinds of pulse in different areas, the barriers to the international trade thereof, and price differentials, there is actually a wider gap between effective supply and demand than this statement would indicate. For example, the surplus of beans in North America, because of shipping, taste and price considerations, is not especially useful to meet the shortage of garbanzos in India. Furthermore, the stocks of beans could be consumed within the bean-consuming areas, together with the estimated 1950-51 production, without exceeding the prewar per capita consumption level in the bean consuming areas.

BEANS, PEAS, LENTILS AND GARBANZOS, DRY EDIBLE: Production by continents,
averages 1935-39.and 1940-44, annual 1948-50

Type and continent	Production				
	Average		Annual		
	1935-39	1940-44	1948	1949	1950 1/
	1,000 bags		1,000 bags		
Beans					
North America......	21,393	26,672	31,605	32,201	25,834
Europe.............	23,525	23,533	22,695	20,399	18,572
Asia...............	37,559	31,551	28,357	28,331	29,386
South America......	21,703	24,860	31,944	31,232	32,380
Africa.............	1,977	1,892	2,495	2,628	2,594
Total...........	106,157	108,508	117,096	114,791	108,766
Peas					
North America......	3,417	7,599	4,558	3,924	3,494
Europe.............	9,447	11,591	10,365	12,024	10,562
Asia...............	55,501	46,248	69,052	62,811	62,787
South America......	711	673	713	674	670
Africa.............	638	870	1,297	1,194	976
Oceania............	509	849	743	688	690
Total...........	70,223	67,830	86,728	81,315	79,179
Lentils					
North America......	22	23	44	35	35
Europe.............	1,282	1,327	1,618	1,330	1,279
Asia...............	1,438	1,628	1,709	1,645	2,080
South America......	850	575	856	774	880
Africa.............	1,337	1,418	1,409	1,583	1,770
Total...........	4,929	4,971	5,636	5,367	6,044
Garbanzos (chickpeas)					
North America......	1,116	1,742	2,628	2,162	2,045
Europe.............	4,441	4,772	3,661	4,719	4,879
Asia...............	2/104,242	2/101,136	116,073	122,349	105,889
South America......	323	220	275	102	108
Africa.............	880	1,179	1,056	1,198	932
Total...........	111,002	109,049	123,693	130,530	113,853
Total pulses 2/..	292,311	290,358	333,153	332,003	307,842

1/ Preliminary.
2/ Official estimates increased by 25 million bags to adjust for areas not
reported by India prior to 1946/47.

EDIBLE FATS AND OILS

World production of edible fats and oils in 1950 reached a new postwar high. Estimated at 21.5 million tons, it exceeded the 1949 output by 2 percent and was 4 percent above prewar. 1/. Although the new high level of production indicates a significant expansion from the previous year, on a per capita basis the world is still short of fats and oils in relation to prewar standards. Production has not kept abreast of increases in the world's population.

Distribution of surplus supplies of fats and oils is still a problem. It is not so serious, however, as it was in previous postwar years. While Western Europe has continued to find it necessary to procure some needed supplies from dollar countries--because of the sharp postwar curtailment of exports by India, China, and Manchuria--the shortage of free dollars is less acute now than a year ago. Consequently, the free-dollar transactions in relation to procurement under dollar-aid programs (Economic Cooperation Administration and Government and Relief in Occupied Areas) are more important today than 12 months ago.

Prices of fats, oils, and oilseeds have risen sharply since mid-1950, principally because of the war in Korea. The price rises have aggravated the problem of procurement of fat supplies from dollar areas by many non-dollar countries eager to supplement their domestic production and imports from other sources.

Trade in edible fats and oils in 1951 is likely to be in large volume. If the Far Eastern countries, traditional surplus suppliers of fats-and-oils materials, should be cut off from world trade, the pressure on supplies in the United States would mount sharply.

Edible Vegetable Oils: The 1950 production of edible vegetable oils—not including the palm oils--is estimated at 9.2 million tons. This is somewhat less than the 9.6 million tons produced in 1949 but is considerably more than the prewar average of nearly 8.4 million tons. Supplies of oil from peanut, soybean, sunflower, and rapeseed crops exceeded prewar by an estimated 1.4 million tons with the greatest percentage increase in sunflower and soybean oils, whereas supplies from cottonseed, olive, and sesame crops declined almost 0.6 million tons with the greatest percentage decrease in olive oil. Compared with 1949, supplies of oil from the 1950

1/ These estimates of production of edible fats and oils include cottonseed, peanut, soybean, olive, sunflower, sesame, and rapeseed (used almost entirely for food), the palm oils, particularly coconut and palm oil (a large proportion of which has gone into food uses in recent years), butter (see page 67), lard, tallow, whale, and fish oils.

peanut, soybean, and rapeseed crops increased by roughly 0.5 million tons
with by far the greatest expansion in soybean oil. Output of cottonseed,
sunflower, olive, and sesame oils was less than in 1949 by some 0.8 million
tons with the decrease in olive oil accounting for two-thirds of the loss.
The only significant increase over 1949 in edible oil crops in North
America occurred in soybeans and peanuts; in South America, cottonseed; in
Europe, cottonseed; in Asia, cottonseed, rapeseed, peanuts, and soybeans;
and in Africa, peanuts.

Supplies of edible oilseeds available for international trade, which
have been particularly low since the war, probably will not reach prewar
volume in 1951, despite the fact that exports the last 2 years showed a
decided increase from previous postwar years.

With the disappearance of Manchurian soybeans from traditional channels
of international trade, the United States has become, and probably will
continue to be, the principal soybean exporter. Shipments of beans and oil
from the United States in 1951 may be no larger than a year earlier, despite a large increase in the crop, due to strong demand for edible oils in
the United States. High prices for soybeans and soybean oil also will dis-
courage exports.

Peanut exports from India, formerly the world's largest exporter, have
been and likely will continue to be negligible in comparison with prewar
average shipments of over one million tons.

. With supplies of cottonseed down from 1949 and from prewar, exports
of cottonseed and oil are not expected to increase.

The reduction in Mediterranean olive oil output by over 0.5 million
tons from 1949 will mean a tighter supply situation and reduced exports.

Sunflower seed oil exports from Argentina may increase in 1951 despite the fact that the 1950 crop was down from 1949. Prospects indicate
increased plantings for harvest in 1951 (April).

Coconut and Palm Oils: Total production of coconut and palm oils in
1950, although still considerably below prewar, is believed to have exceeded 1949 output by nearly 0.1 million tons. Coconut oil production
increased slightly—primarily the result of expansion in Philippine production. Malayan output may have maintained the 1949 level, but production in Indonesia and Ceylon dropped considerably. Availabilities in 1951
for importing countries will be determined largely by international developments.

Production in 1950 of palm oil and palm kernel oil increased considerably over 1949 and over prewar. Continued expansion in the Belgian Congo
and Indonesia should increase the volume for international trade in 1951.

Animal Fats: World production of animal fats--lard, tallow, and butter--in 1950 reached and surpassed the prewar level for the first time since the war. Output last year is estimated at 8.7 million tons. This represents an increase of 6 percent from 1949, and nearly 5 percent from prewar. Most of the gain from 1949 resulted from increases in the output of lard--in the United States and Europe--and gains in the output of butter particularly in Europe. Butter production (fat content) in 1950 exceeded an estimated 3.4 million tons, 11 percent more than in 1949.

Production in the United States of lard and tallow in 1950 was higher than in 1949, and output is expected to increase again in 1951. Butter production in the United States, down somewhat in 1950 from 1949, is expected to decline further in 1951.

Animal fats production throughout the world is likely to be greater in 1951 than in the last year.

Marine Oils: Production in 1950 of marine oils--which consist of whale (excluding sperm) and fish oils (excluding liver oils)--is estimated at nearly 0.8 million tons. This quantity is 9 percent more than the output in 1949 but is equivalent to only three-fourths the tonnage produced in prewar years.

Whale oil production in 1950 is estimated at more than 0.4 million tons, a slight gain from 1949. Output of this oil, of which the dominant share comes from whales caught in the Southern Hemisphere during the Antarctic pelagic season, continues to be restricted by the catch limitations imposed under the International Whaling Convention of 1946. Consequently, production of this oil, used extensively in Europe in the production of margarine, is not expected to rise materially in 1951.

Fish oil output in 1950 is estimated at somewhat more than 0.3 million tons, an increase of 20 percent from production in 1949. Although this estimated tonnage is still fully one-fourth below prewar levels, the generally higher price level likely to obtain in the current year may stimulate further increases in the production of fish oil.

COFFEE

The decrease of about 2 percent in world coffee production forecast for 1950-51 is chiefly attributable to the smaller Brazilian harvest which resulted from extremely dry weather during the flowering season. Brazil normally provides more than half of the world's coffee supply. The amount of coffee from Brazil's 1950 harvest available for export during 1950-51 is estimated at only 13,600,000 bags, compared with 14,950,000 bags in 1949-50, and an annual prewar average of 21,740,000 bags.

The smaller coffee crop forecast for South America is only partially offset by higher forecasts for Africa and Asia. Coffee production in North America and Oceania is expected to approximate the 1949-50 output. A significant increase is expected in Mexico, where the Government has embarked upon an ambitious undertaking greatly to expand the coffee industry. In Africa coffee production has practically doubled since prewar years. Indonesia, Asia's leading coffee growing country, was the third most important coffee producing country in prewar years, but is declined considerably during the war. Coffee production now is expanding rapidly, but it is not likely that Indonesia will regain its prewar position in the world coffee market.

CACAO

World production of cacao beans in 1950-51 is forecast at 1,687 million pounds, only a little lower than the record output in 1949-50 and about 7 percent higher than annual prewar average (1935-36/1939-40) production. All except a relatively small quantity of the cacao beans produced in 1950-51 will be available for export, since consumption in most producing countries is very low.

It should be emphasized that the forecast of 1950-51 cacao production is highly tentative as the harvesting season in many countries has just begun, and the final outturn will depend on the weather, diseases, prices, labor supply, and other factors. Also, large amounts of cacao in marginal producing areas very often are unharvested because of labor shortages or unattractive prices. Current prices paid to cacao producers are relatively favorable.

The slight decrease in world cacao production forecast for 1950-51 is chiefly attributable to the much smaller output expected in Brazil. Brazil harvested a record crop of around 355 million pounds of cacao beans in 1949-50, but unfavorable weather and the normal tendency of cacao trees to "rest" following an unusually heavy yield are expected to reduce the 1950-51 output to around 275 million pounds. Increases in production in certain other areas, however, practically offset the decline in Brazil.

The most significant increase in cacao production is forecast for the Gold Coast. The Gold Coast's main crop has been officially forecast at about 605 million pounds. Assuming a normal mid-crop (harvested from May to June) of 20 million pounds, the Gold Coast is expected to produce about 625 million pounds of cacao beans in 1950-51. This compares with an output of 572 million pounds in 1949-50, and an annual prewar average production of 609 million pounds.

MEAT

World production of meat is currently about 10 percent above the prewar level but per capita meat consumption is 5 percent below prewar level as the population since 1940 has increased significantly.

The world meat output in 1950 is placed at 6 percent above the 1949 level and a further increase of approximately this magnitude is expected in 1951. This follows a 5 percent increase in output in 1949 over 1948 and will bring the increase to 19 percent in the three years ending with 1951. These increases in meat supply have resulted from the restoration of Western European herds, exceedingly strong consumer demand, and favorable grazing and feed situations.

The 1950 world meat output of 72.7 billion pounds when compared with the 1949 output represents about 3 percent more beef and veal and 12 percent more pork but about 5 percent less mutton and lamb and 5 percent less goat and horse meat. At the same time, livestock inventories on January 1, 1950 were up 1 per cent for cattle, 7 percent for hogs and 1 percent for sheep over January 1, 1949. Further increases are likely to be shown by 1951 inventories when compiled.

In evaluating these trends in livestock numbers and meat supplies the fact should be borne in mind that the past 3 years have been generally favorable for crop and forage production. Future trends in livestock numbers and meat production will depend upon the extent to which herds might have to be reduced or could be increased in keeping with feed supplies.

An appreciable part of the increase in meat supplies in recent years is accounted for by the expanded pork production made possible by abundant grain supplies. A recent hog slaughter survey of the principal producing countries indicates that commercial or inspected hog slaughter in 1950 was almost 30 percent above prewar and that a further increase of at least 7 percent is expected in 1951. This level of hog production cuts heavily into feed grain supplies.

Notwithstanding the higher level of meat output in 1950 and early 1951, meat prices have gradually worked higher. High levels of business activity and consumer incomes, together with increases in population, have exerted pressure upon the demand side. This has been especially true in North America and in Western Europe.

Meat output in North America increased only slightly in 1950 with the production of pork more than offsetting the decline in beef and veal and mutton and lamb. The output in Europe increased sharply and accounts for nearly all the gain in world output. In Europe the output of both beef and pork increased sharply with other meats remaining about the same. South American production increased slightly with higher output in Brazil and Uruguay but with a lower output in Argentina. Meat production in 1950 in Australia decreased slightly but was nearly offset by a larger output in New Zealand.

In 1949, approximately 6 percent of the world meat production moved in international trade. A smaller proportion is believed to have moved in 1950 as exports from Argentina were sharply curtailed in the latter half of the year. That country in recent years has exported about one-third of the meat entering world trade. A decreasing preportion of the Argentine output is now available for export. The domestic market in that country took 75 percent of the output in 1949 compared with only 60 percent of the output in the prewa period.

Canada and Mexico also reduced their exports of meat in 1950 compared wit. 1949. Denmark, Uruguay, Australia and New Zealand were the other principal exporters in 1950. All exported larger quantities in 1950 than in the previous year but Denmark showed the greatest increase. Exports from that country approached the quantities exported in the prewar period.

The supply of meat per capita in the United Kingdom, the principal meat importing country, is approximately 75 percent of prewar. While the output of domestically produced meat in that country has been rapidly approaching prewar, other importing countries are competing strongly for the reduced supplies available from exporting countries. The United States, Germany and Belgium are the other principal importing countries. Imports of meats into the United States in 1950 are expected to total 400 million pounds (carcass weight equivalent) compared with 242 million pounds in 1949. The acquisition of meat from abroad by the United Kingdom has been further aggravated by a disagreement on the price to be paid to Argentina for meat. Shipments to the United Kingdom from that country have been suspended since July 21, 1950. A similar disagreement exists in the case of shipments from Uruguay to the United Kingdom.

MEAT 1/: PRODUCTION, NET TRADE AND CONSUMPTION, PREWAR AND
ESTIMATED PRODUCTION AND EXPORT SUPPLIES, 1950

Country	Prewar 2/				Preliminary 1950	
	Production	Net Exports	Net Imports	Apparent Consumption	Production	Gross Exports
	Mil. lbs.	Mil. lbs	Mil.lbs	Mil. lbs	Mil. lbs.	Mil. lbs.
Canada	1,417	168		1,223	1,920	160
Mexico	698		1	699	1,000	50
United States	16,182		65	16,382	22,400	
Cuba	309		4	313	410	
Austria	617		13	630	440	
Belgium	693		48	741	695	
Bulgaria	337	6		331	--	
Czechoslovakia	944	3/		944	--	
Denmark 4/	1,105	572		504	1,100	525
Finland	254	5		249	235	
France	4,015		48	4,063	4,100	100
Western Germany	4,140				3,525	
Greece	208		3	211	170	
Hungary	538	18		520	--	
Ireland	336	71		265	350	50
Italy	1,542		115	1,657	1,535	
Luxembourg	40					
Netherlands	894	65		829	870	70
Norway	223		2	225	250	
Poland	2,450				--	90
Portugal	290		3/	290	350	
Rumania	657	6		651	--	
Sweden	649	16		633	680	
Switzerland	419		17	436	390	
United Kingdom	2,850		3,422	6,272	2,400	
Yugoslavia	888	19		869	--	
Soviet Union	7,292		3	7,295	--	
Argentina 5/	4,459	1,460		2,999	5,250	1,000
Brazil 6/	2,214	211		2,003	2,825	50
Chile	349	18		331	420	10
Paraguay 7/	167	16		151	225	30
Uruguay 6/	581	324		257	680	350
Union of S.Africa	671		6	677	950	
Australia	2,202	521		1,680	2,230	600
New Zealand	1,024	600		424	1,250	800

1/ Carcass meat basis-includes beef and veal, pork, mutton and lamb, goat and
horse meat. Excludes edible offal and lard. 2/ Prewar is average for years 1935-39
for United States, Canada, Sweden and Denmark; 1936-38 for New Zealand and the
United Kingdom; 1936 for Czechoslovakia, 1938 for Poland and Soviet Union; and
1934-38 principally for other countries. 3/ Less than 500,000 pounds. 4/ Includes
c.w.e. of live cattle exported. 5/Excludes farm production and consumption of
pork. 6/Excludes farm production. 7/ Beef and veal only.

OFFICE OF FOREIGN AGRICULTURAL RELATIONS, 1/11/51

DAIRY PRODUCTS

Milk output in most countries of the world continued to increase during 1950. In the reporting countries output is tentatively estimated at 8 percent above prewar (1934-38), but the total world production is estimated at approxi mately the prewar level. Milk production in the principal dairy countries is expected to increase again in 1951 but at a somewhat slower rate. The expandi mobilization effort in the countries consuming the major portion of the world' supply of dairy products probably will strengthen the market for milk and stim late its production provided the availability of feed and labor permit.

The large milk supply during 1950 resulted from an increase in the number of dairy cows in many countries and an increase in the average production per cow due to better feeding. Milk cow numbers during 1950 increased in all countries where information is available except Australia and the United State Grain and roughage are in fair to good supply, but in several countries the quality of feed on hand is below average. Over the last two years milk has been produced under better-than-average growing conditions for pastures and forage crops. Pasture lands are probably in better condition now than at any time since World War II.

Excess stocks of butter and cheese have practically disappeared. The stocks of nonfat dry milk in the United States are the only large surplus stocks of dairy products that now exist. If there is any surplus of dairy products in 1951 it will be nonfat dry milk.

The per capita consumption of milk and dairy products in most countries is near or above prewar. Several Eastern European countries, not under the European Recovery Program, are still considerably below prewar levels. The consumption of dairy products in many of the Western European countries is approximately the same as in the United States and will continue to make moderate gains during 1951. The per capita consumption of dairy products in the United States will continue to increase above its present relatively high level. The importance of milk as a food has not increased much in most of Asia, but in several South American countries its consumption is rising.

The largest percentage increase in milk production in 1950 continued to be in Europe. The Netherlands, Czechoslovakia, Denmark, Sweden, Ireland, Austria and the United Kingdom all made substantial gains in 1950 over their respective outputs of a year earlier. The United Kingdom, the Netherlands, Norway and Sweden, now are producing milk at levels considerably above prewar.

Milk production in Australia during 1950 was about the same as in 1949 but in New Zealand it was 4.5 percent higher than 1949 and 1 percent above the record year 1940-41. Milk output in the United States gained slightly in 1950 over last year, while Canadian production was a little lower.

In the Caribbean and South American countries, milk production increased as the result of considerable effort by many countries to supply a larger portion of their domestic demands from indigenous production. In Argentina pastures and grazing conditions are much more favorable this season than a year ago.

Butter production in the world during 1950 is tentatively estimated at 8.5 billion pounds or approximately 7 percent above a year earlier but still about 12 percent below prewar (1934-38). The recovery of butter output from the depressed wartime levels has been slow because it has been more profitable to market milk as fluid milk and in other manufactured products that utilize a greater proportion of the whole milk. Also, the consumption of butter has been partially replaced in a number of countries by other edible fats and oils. Supplies of edible fats and oils available to European countries, however, are still somewhat limited.

The increases in butter production during 1950 were principally in the dairy countries of Western Europe, although several of these countries still are below their prewar levels. The United Kingdom continued to be the largest importer, but large quantities were purchased also by Western Germany, Belgium, France, Switzerland, and Italy.

Cheese production in the world continued at a level considerably higher than prewar. The United States, by far the largest producer of cheese in the world, lowered its production during 1950. Only a small part of the 1951 output will be exported and imports may be much higher than in 1950. Production of cheese in Denmark in 1950 was 5 percent below 1949 and other major producing countries such as the Netherlands, Switzerland, and Canada lowered their output, also. The United Kingdom was one of the few countries to show an increase in the manufacture of cheese last year. New Zealand, the Netherlands, Denmark, Australia, Switzerland and Italy, continued to export large quantities of cheese.

Production of canned and dried milk is concentrated in the United States, Canada, the Netherlands, the United Kingdom, Denmark, Australia and New Zealand. The output of these products in the United States and Canada is still very high, and in Western Europe it is recovering rapidly. The supplies available in 1951 should be adequate for levels of consumption above last year. A significant portion of the production of these concentrated milk products is produced for export markets not only to countries where dairy products are widely used but also to a number of tropical and Asiatic markets where indigenous milk supplies are scarce and facilities for handling more perishable milk products are not generally available. The larger production of canned milk in 1950 was due to increases in the United States, Canada, the United Kingdom and the Netherlands.

The changes in production of dried milk in the world during 1950 varied greatly by country. The Netherlands and the United Kingdom both increased their output in 1950 while Sweden's output decreased. The United States and Canada increased the output of dry whole milk but decreased their manufacture of nonfat dry milk which is produced in much larger quantities. The facilities for producing nonfat dry milk and the available supply of skim milk greatly exceed the demand even at prices lower than the cost of production even though nonfat dry milk is a relatively inexpensive food based on its nutritive value.

EGGS

The production of eggs during 1950 by major producing countries 1/ is estimated at approximately 5 percent above 1949 and 30% above the prewar (1935-39) average due largely to the higher output in the United States. The output of eggs in 1951 will be about the same or slightly lower with increases in some European countries nearly offsetting declines in the United States and Canada. The supply, however, will probably be better distributed in 1951 than last year since more eg s will be produced in Europe where the per capita consumption is still largely below prewar and the decrease in production by the United States will be largely offset by the discontinuance of government purchases and storage of dried whole eggs to support domestic prices. In addition the development of the emergency mobilization activity will tend to encourage a higher production of eggs where economically feasible from the birds now available. It will probably also stimulate an increase in the hatch during 1951 particularly for the production of poultry meat as the supply of "red" meats continues short. The high price of feed will, however, temper these tendencies.

The 1950 increase in the supply of eggs was the result both of larger chicken numbers in almost every country, and the better rate-of-lay in a number of countries due to the improved quality of birds and better feeding.

The production of eggs in the United States during 1950 is estimated at 4.5 percent above 1949 while Canadian production is estimated at slightly over 3 percent. The United States which has been the only country to accumulate a large surplus of egg products in the postwar period is unlikely to produce much in excess of domestic consumption during 1951. As government purchases of dried whole eggs have been discontinued these stocks should decrease. Canada successfully adjusted its production to its domestic market in 1950 and will not have eggs in any quantity for export this year.

Practically all Western European countries made large gains in egg production during 1950. The Netherlands egg production in 1950 is estimated at about 22 percent above 1949 and Denmarks 13 percent. Smaller gains were made in Ireland, Sweden, Switzerland, Norway, and France. Most of these countries are likely to have even smaller gains in 1951.

The United Kingdom and Western Germany where significant increases in production occurred, also imported large quantities of eggs, mostly from the Netherlands, Denmark, Australia, Ireland and Poland.

Production in 1950 in several Eastern European countries was the largest since World War II and is expected to increase further in 1951.

The production of eggs in Australia and New Zealand is not expected to change much in 1951 from last year.

1/ Excludes Soviet Union and China

Lightning Source UK Ltd.
Milton Keynes UK
UKHW010906231118
332790UK00007B/216/P